OSPREY/**AIRWAR** SERIES   EDITOR: MARTIN WINDROW

RAF BOMBER UNITS
JULY 1942-1945

BY BRYAN PHILPOTT

COLOUR PLATES BY
TERRY HADLER
RICHARD HOOK

OSPREY PUBLISHING LONDON

Published in 1978 by
Osprey Publishing Ltd
Member company of the George Philip Group
12–14 Long Acre, London WC2E 9LP
© Copyright 1978 Osprey Publishing Ltd

ISBN 0 85045 293 7

Unless otherwise credited, all photographs are courtesy of the
Imperial War Museum.

Filmset by BAS Printers Limited, Over Wallop,
Hampshire, England
Printed in Hong Kong

NEW WEAPONS

When Air Marshal A. T. Harris took over the reins at Bomber Command Headquarters in February 1942, he inherited a force of some 400 aircraft—100 fewer than had been available to his predecessor the previous December, when he had been ordered to limit operations during the winter months. The first task facing the new Commander in Chief was to silence the growing criticism which threatened the very existence of his force in a strategic bombing role. Harris, who had been a firm advocate of precision bombing, soon appreciated that this was beyond the capability of the crews and aircraft then available to him, and quickly became a champion of area bombing. This does not mean that he was in any way a 'yes man' or armchair leader ready to abandon his own theories in favour of those of his seniors. The truth was, in fact, quite the reverse, for he was a capable leader who, although ready to defend and stick resolutely to his own views through thick and thin, could appreciate others' opinions and adopt them if, in his opinion, they merited it. Having decided on a course of action, Harris would pursue it to its fulfilment, which on occasions made him unpopular with both his seniors and members of the government.

The change in policy to area bombing—in which whole towns, rather than individual factories or industrial areas, became the prime objective of the bombers—placed the German civilian population firmly in the front line. Towns and cities supporting nearby industrial complexes became earmarked for special attention. The destruction of homes, the cutting off of gas, water and electricity supplies, as well as creating breakdowns in communications, would, it was believed, lead to absenteeism on a mammoth scale, thus effectively disrupting production. The raid on Lübeck on the night of 28 March 1942 was typical of the new policy; three-quarters of the attacking force of 191 aircraft had

The Short Stirling was the first British four-engined bomber to enter service when No. 7 Sqn. received examples in 1941. These six machines of No. 7 Sqn. were photographed at their base, Oakington, late that year. Worthy of note are the small size unit codes 'MG', aircraft 'M', 'A', 'Y', 'Z', 'B' and 'W' being visible.

carried incendiaries and the raid resulted in the devastation of 200 acres. This was Bomber Command's first real success in area bombing, and if the critics still had doubts, the first of three 1,000 bomber raids on Cologne two months later finally silenced them.

The accolades that were heaped onto Harris after the Cologne raid put him in a position of strength when it came to his repeated requests for more bombers, more crews and electronic equipment. The success of this raid however, had more far-reaching consequences, for it was the first time that a bomber 'stream' was used.

In addition to this new tactic, in which all aircraft flew the same route to and from the target as well as being allocated individual heights and space within the stream, an experiment in limiting time over the target was also tried. By doing this the duration of the attack was reduced but the concentration was increased, resulting in ground defences and facilities such as fire-fighting services being overwhelmed by continually growing demands. The result of the use of the bomber stream in a concentrated attack was that the duration of the 1,000 bomber raid was one and a half hours as against the two hours taken by the 191 aircraft which had attacked Lübeck. A further bonus, which more than offset the considerably increased risk of collision between bombers operating in such close proximity, was the concentrated penetration of the German night-fighter control system.

By 1942 the Luftwaffe had established an efficient fighter control network based on the use of long and short-range radar, as well as zoned areas. All approaches to Germany were divided into 'boxes' in which a radar-controlled fighter would orbit a radio beacon. When approaching bombers were located by long-range radar, the pilot would be warned. Shorter range but more accurate *Würzburg* radar would then be used to locate the exact position of the bomber and fighter, and a ground controller would vector the two plots to an intercepting position. By concentrating the whole bomber force in one stream the RAF hoped that the Luftwaffe ground controllers' radar screens would become saturated and unable to pick out individual targets. Only those 'boxes' through which the stream was flying could be brought into action, so in many areas night fighters would be left orbiting uselessly.

This early use of the bomber stream was immediately vindicated since it achieved every objective expected, and from it grew the basic tactics that became standard in the years to come. Naturally counter-measures by both sides brought the necessity of change as the bombing war progressed, but the foundations on which a sound strategic bombing policy could be built were laid over Cologne.

No. 7 Sqn. Stirlings being bombed-up for the night's work.

The success of the first 1,000 bomber raid was not repeated over Essen, where cloud and industrial smog made target location difficult and bombs fell over a wide area, causing comparatively little damage. The two raids, and the one against Bremen on 25/26 June, proved that given the aircraft, Harris was capable of mounting a full-scale campaign. But aircraft were at a premium in the spring of 1942, and even if they had been available in the quantities the C-in-C wanted them, the supply of crews would have been a bigger problem.

Aircraft such as the Wellington, Whitley and Hampden, which had borne the brunt of the bomber offensive since 1939, were outdated, and the flow of the new four-engined heavies was still but a trickle. Even if these aircraft had been available at this time in greater quantity, the men to crew them would not: whereas the twins of the early war years had needed a five-man crew, the Halifax, Stirling and Lancaster needed seven and until the flow of new aircrew from the training schools got under way, manpower shortage was one of the major problems facing Bomber Command. Harris was also frustrated by the drain of trained

No. 149 Sqn. Stirlings being prepared for operations. The two airmen are wearing red arm bands with the word ARMOURY in dark blue on their left sleeves. The aircraft in the foreground, OJ-N, is having a final engine test before its bombs are loaded.

crews to the Middle East, over 1,000 being transferred to the Desert Air Force during the opening months of 1942. So although the successes of Lübeck, Cologne, Essen and Bremen, had led Churchill into describing Bomber Command as 'our immensely powerful weapon', its strength was somewhat illusory and it would not be until 1943 that Harris had the equipment and men at his disposal to mount the offensive he planned.

However, in the force attacking Cologne had been sixty-eight of the new Lancaster bombers which had entered service in late 1941 and flew their first operation on 3 March 1942. In the Lancaster, Harris knew that he had the weapon *par excellence*. Such was his confidence in it that, barely a month after its operational début over Germany (an attack on Essen on 10 March) Harris used it to mount a daring daylight raid deep in enemy territory.

Although the new C-in-C had been given a clear

STIRLING SQUADRONS

Squadron	Code	Date type first received
7	MG	Aug 1940
15	LS	Apr 1941
75	AA	Nov 1942
90	WP/XY*	Nov 1942
149	OJ/TK*	Nov 1941
196	ZO	Jul 1943
199	EX	Jul 1943
214	BU/PX*	Apr 1942
218	HA	Jan 1942
622	GI	Aug 1943
623	IC	Aug 1943

*'C' Flt codes.

Halifax B.II coded LQ-Q of No. 405 (Vancouver) Sqn., RCAF at Topcliffe in 1942. This squadron flew the first RCAF bombing raid in June 1941 with Wellingtons and was re-equipped with the Halifax in time to take part in the first 1,000 bomber raid.

directive by the Air Ministry to mount an area bombing campaign against industrial towns, the occasional pin-point attack against selected targets had not been ruled out, and in this Harris saw an ideal opportunity to try his new weapon.

The mounting toll of shipping to U-boats in the Atlantic at that time gave cause for considerable concern. In the submarine, Germany had a weapon which could still bring Britain to her knees, and if this happened, there would be no base from which the proposed Anglo-American bomber offensive could be mounted, and perhaps more important in 1942, no starting point for a second front. The Americans, who had entered the war in December 1941, were busily occupied in the Pacific, so could do little at this stage to help combat the U-boat; but as losses continued to mount, especially along the Atlantic coast where over three quarters of a million tons of shipping were sunk in the first two months of 1942, President Roosevelt called on Churchill to take some decisive British action.

Bomber Command's experiences in the first two

The crew of Halifax B.II LQ-Q of No. 405 (Vancouver) Sqn. leave their crew bus to take their positions on board.

years of the war had proved that daylight operations were suicidal with the aircraft then available, and claims of bombing accuracy to within a few hundred yards were grossly exaggerated. To find a strategic target such as a submarine yard or factory at night, then bomb it accurately, was out of the question; so Harris found himself confronted with a problem in which he saw the Lancaster as the solution—the speed, range and armament of the four-engined bomber, might just enable the impossible to be achieved. He instructed his planning staff to select a target, the destruction of which would put a severe brake on U-boat production. Harris, who had originally been a strong advocate of precision bombing, but had by now become as fierce a champion of area bombing, was bitterly opposed to attacking what became known as 'panacea' targets; that is those whose destruction would, it was believed, have an immediate effect on some aspect of Germany's ability to wage war. Nonetheless, he could not ignore the pressing demands for such a raid on this occasion, as he did not have sufficient forces available to produce the desired cut-back in U-boat production by mass attack.

The target finally selected was the MAN diesel

A Stirling testing its four ·303in Browning tail guns in the firing butts.

A Halifax bomb-aimer in his position in the nose of the aircraft. Bomb selector switches are on the small console to his right.

The rear gunner of Halifax B.II LQ-Q demonstrates one method of entry through the rear doors. In the event of having to bale out, it was recommended that the gunner swivelled his turret into this position and rolled out backwards. The gunner is wearing a flying suit with a 'woolly' texture, a Mae West and chest type parachute harness.

The mid-upper gunner of a No. 9 Sqn. Lancaster. (via R. Leask-Ward)

engine works at Augsburg which was believed to be supplying over half the total requirement of engines for submarines, warships and AFVs. Nos. 44 (Rhodesia) and 97 Squadrons, the first to receive Lancasters, were selected to provide twelve aircraft. At briefing on the morning of 17 April 1942, crews could hardly believe their eyes as the target route was revealed—it meant a 500-mile trip over hostile territory in broad daylight, to bomb a single factory with four 1,000lb bombs per aircraft. There was some consolation in the fact that Bostons, under huge fighter escort, would simultaneously attack Luftwaffe airfields in France and attempt to divert German fighters away from the Lancasters.

Led by Squadron Leader John Nettleton, the bombers roared over France, their unusually low altitude a further ruse to catch the Germans napping, but it was not to be. Bf109s and Fw190s shot down four of Nettleton's section of six aircraft.

Heavy flak greeted the attackers over the target: one Lancaster went down on the run-in, two crashed in the target area and after bombing, the five tattered survivors limped home. Although the MAN works was damaged, production was only slightly curtailed, and the loss of seven bombers and forty-nine crewmen was a severe price to pay. Any hopes of further pin-point attacks after the 17 April raid were dashed when it was made clear that even the Lancaster could not survive in enemy airspace in daylight without fighter protection, which was just not available at that time. For his leadership on the Augsburg raid, Sqn. Ldr. Nettleton was awarded a Victoria Cross, the first of ten to go to Lancaster crew members.

Another aircraft which was to play a significant part in Bomber Command's offensive was the de Havilland Mosquito, which entered the arena on the morning after the 1,000 bomber raid on Cologne, when four aircraft of No. 105 Sqn. visited the city. Leaving their base at Horsham St Faith at intervals over several hours, three of the Mosquitoes found Cologne so obscured by smoke and clouds that they could only bomb on dead reckoning and were unable to observe the results of their efforts. One aircraft failed to return.

The Lancaster and Mosquito have, quite rightly, received much praise for the work they carried out in Bomber Command, but their achievements have often been allowed to overshadow the not inconsiderable contribution made by the other two four-

A close-up of the faired nose of a Halifax B.II Srs 1 (Special) (via R. Leask-Ward)

The pilot and flight engineer of a Lancaster of No. 9 Sqn., December 1942. (via R. Leask-Ward)

Unique nose art on Halifax B.II W7710/LQ-R of No. 405 (Vancouver) Sqn., RCAF. The crew added another truck after each raid, and the small figure at the front of the cavalcade is saying 'Hey Goering, R-Robert is here again'.

engined heavies, the Stirling and Halifax. Both these aircraft were a disappointment in their first year of service—in fact it would be quite true to claim that the former was handicapped from the start by its comparatively poor performance, especially in service ceiling—but the latter, after overcoming aerodynamic problems, blossomed into a very workmanlike aircraft much liked and respected by the men who crewed it. In fact there are still many Halifax crew members who will willingly extol its virtues, and putting aside their natural enthusiastic rivalry, compare it very favourably with the Lancaster. The general opinion among ex-bomber crews is that the Stirling and Halifax could take a lot more punishment than the Lancaster, and certainly gave their crews a better chance of

A Halifax B.II Srs 1 (Special) of No. 10 Sqn. This type of Halifax had the front turret removed and was frequently used for special duties. The aircraft illustrated, BB324, was lost in June 1943. (via R. Leask-Ward)

survival in forced landings. One wireless operator, Pilot Officer C. J. Phillips, can speak authoritatively on this subject, as he flew in and experienced wheels-up landings in both types: his Mk III Halifax stayed reasonably intact with none of the crew injured, whilst his Lancaster broke in half and several crew members suffered serious cuts and broken limbs.

In April 1942 the new aircraft category of 'Air Bomber' was introduced and observers were renamed navigators, giving a seven man bomber crew a new composition of pilot, navigator, flight engineer, bomb-aimer, wireless operator, and two air gunners. In many cases the bomb-aimer was an ex-trainee pilot who for one reason or another had failed to complete his course—a bonus that was to stand many a crew in good stead when the regular pilot was killed or injured.

Navigation, which had not been a strong point in the opening years of the war, now took a turn for the better, and with the introduction of navigational aids such as 'Gee'—first used in March 1942—and H2S, the crews had a much better chance of finding their targets, hitting them hard, and finding their way home. One other major event of 1942, which was to play a most important part in the bomber offensive, was the formation of the Pathfinder Force (PFF).

Since 1941 experienced crews had advocated that the finding and illumination of targets by specialist crews could only lead to greater destruction by the remaining bombers; in fact on some raids Wellingtons had carried a high proportion of incendiaries with this purpose in mind. Harris was against the formation of an élite force of squadrons to undertake this task and in this was supported by some of his group commanders. One argument put forward by those against the idea was that by taking experienced crews away from their squadrons, morale would suffer. This was not supported by those in favour of the move who were always ready to point out that it was not their intention to form a *corps d'élite*.

Group Captain S. O. Bufton, a former CO of Nos.

10 and 76 Sqns., with much operational experience to call upon, and then Deputy Director of Bomber Operations at Air Ministry, was very enthusiastic about a marking force and eventually persuaded the Air Staff to form one within Bomber Command. Harris was instructed to create it.

The C-in-C, although not opposed to target marking as such, and arguing that selected squadrons within each group could perform this task, was initially upset that a staff officer of junior rank should interfere with his work, but he accepted his directive with good grace and typically backed his new force to the hilt. Having accepted the task set him, Harris wasted no time in appointing Wing Commander D. R. Bennett to command the PFF which came into being on 16 August. Bennett was the ideal man to undertake the job; a superb pilot and expert navigator who had commanded Nos. 10 and 77 Sqns., he had flown on many operations including an attack on the *Tirpitz* in Foetten Fjord on 27/28 April, during which his Halifax had been shot down and he had escaped through Sweden.

The nucleus of PFF, in which all crews were volunteers and had to complete 50 trips as opposed to the normal 30, was Nos. 156, 7, 35, 83 and 109 Sqns., which were assembled on 17 August and ordered by Harris to be ready for operations that night. In the event, bad weather cancelled the first operation but the force had only a short respite, for the following evening it flew to Flensburg. This was something of an anti-climax, as thick cloud obscured the target and made visual marking impossible. The PFF came in for criticism from those opposed to it, but it was not too long before the critics were made to eat their words as the main bomber offensive got under way, with pathfinder units doing all that was asked of them.

A Lancaster of No. 83 Sqn. undergoing final checks before receiving its load. This aircraft was formerly with No. 44 Sqn. whose codes 'KM' can be seen under the freshly painted 'OL' codes of No. 83. The ground crew are adding their own chalk slogans to the waiting bombs, the one in the foreground being marked 'ONE FROM LONDON', and the one on the left, 'TO ADOLF WITH LOVE'.

Two Polish air gunners at a training school prepare for the day's work. Both men are wearing the integral type life jacket and parachute harness and carrying drums of ammunition, as well as belted rounds.

Air gunners under training—denoted by the white flash in the two outer figures' side caps—with their English instructor—the second man from the right is Polish and on the left and right are two Czech cadets. All three are wearing Sidcot suits and brown leather gauntlet gloves.

AREA BOMBING

After the three 1,000 bomber raids in the spring of 1942, Bomber Command gradually began to build its strength in both personnel and aircraft. The stream technique was now standard practice, and as navigation improved, the somewhat 'hit-and-miss' days of the first two and a half years of the war began to recede. Twin-engined light bombers were still forming the major part of the command's strike force, but gradually the Whitley, Hampden and Wellington were being phased out for the Stirling, Halifax and Lancaster. The Whitley was the first to go, being officially withdrawn in April, but in fact continuing to operate on special duties and with OCUs in the bomber stream for several months. The Hampden soldiered on until September 1942 and the Wellington gave legion service in the bombing rôle until October 1943.

The U-boat menace caused concern throughout 1942, and in June six Lancasters of No. 44 Sqn. were loaned to Coastal Command for anti-submarine patrols, operating with No. 15 Group from Nutts Corner in Northern Ireland. During the month's detachment the Lancasters attacked two U-boats, one of which, U-552, was claimed as sunk.

Although new crews were entering the command, Harris was still unable to mount the full-scale offensives he planned, and secondments such as that of No. 44 Sqn. did not help the overall situation. In June and July attacks were mounted against Bremen, Duisberg, Hamburg, Dusseldorf and Danzig. The latter was another attempt to disrupt U-boat production and was mounted by forty Lancasters from Nos. 83, 97, 106 and 207 Sqns., which flew at low level but failed to find their main objective. They returned less three of their number, having dropped their bombs on enemy shipping. On the last day of July a force of over 500 bombers including 104 Lancasters—the first time over 100 of this type had operated together—made a successful attack on the Scheiss AG works at Dusseldorf. The clear weather and a bright moon made target location relatively easy and considerable damage was caused to one of the largest machine-tool works in Germany.

Despite its failure to mark Flensburg on the night

of 18/19 August, PFF was confident that it could successfully guide the mass of bombers collectively termed Main Force to the designated target, and illuminate that target effectively. Raids on Kassal and Nuremberg on 27/28 and 28/29 August, in which special incendiaries were used by PFF, brought the results hoped for and proved immensely valuable to the main attacking force. At this time PFF was using basically the same type of incendiary as Main Force aircraft, but in an attempt to distinguish pathfinder incendiaries, the casings were filled with rubber and phosphorus and used purely as a guide : Main Force still had to identify its own aiming point.

In early 1943 special target indicators were available and a policy of bombing these was soon adopted as PFF became more proficient at finding and marking. One of the earliest type of specialized marker was a 4,000lb MC bomb casing filled with a mixture of benzol, rubber and phosphorus, coloured so that it burned with a pink hue. Known as 'Pink Pansy', it was used for the first time on 10/11 September over Dusseldorf, which was also marked with green and red flares to its east and west boundaries. The attacking force used the flares to approach the target, then bombed the Pink Pansies, causing huge fires and devastation in the town.

The techniques to be used by PFF in 1943/44 were being developed at this time, as were methods of marking the target and the means of getting such markers accurately to their destination. One of the earliest systems used, which became fairly standard practice, was the splitting of the force into three categories; the Illuminators arrived first and identified the target, then came the Primary Visual Markers which marked the aiming point, and finally, the Backers-up, whose task was to drop incendiary bombs on the target markers. The navigational aid Gee was obviously one answer to accurate target location, but soon after PFF was formed, the Germans found an effective method of jamming it. However, two more electronic aids were soon to become available, as the pendulum of measure and counter-measure swung back in favour of Bomber Command. The first of these was 'Oboe', which strictly speaking was more of a target location device than a navigational one. It relied on two beams transmitted from ground stations in

HALIFAX SQUADRONS

Squadron	Code	First received
10	ZA	Dec 1941
35	TL	Nov 1940
51	MH/LK†/C6‡	Nov 1942
76	MP	May 1941
77	KN	Dec 1942
78	EY	Mar 1942
102	DY	Dec 1941
103	PM	Jul 1942
158	NP	Jun 1942
178	?	May 1943
346	H7	May 1944
347	L8	Jun 1944
405	LQ	Apr 1942
408	EQ	Oct 1942
415	6U	Jul 1944
419	VR	Nov 1942
420	PT	Dec 1943
424	QB	Dec 1943
425	KW	Dec 1943
426	OW	Apr 1944
427	ZL	May 1943
428	NA	Jun 1943
429	AL	Aug 1943
431	SE	Jul 1943
432	QO	Feb 1944
433	BM	Nov 1943
434	IP	Jun 1943
460	UV/AR*	Aug 1942
462	Z5	Aug 1942
466	HD	Sep 1943
578	LK	Jan 1944
614	?	Mar 1944
640	C8	Jan 1944

† 'C' Flt codes
‡ 'C' Flt codes. Became nucleus of No. 578 Sqn.
* Possibly only used on squadron's Lancasters.

MANCHESTER SQUADRONS

Squadron	Code	First received
49	EA	Apr 1942
50	VN	Apr 1942
61	QR	Jun 1941
83	OL	Jan 1942
97	OF	Feb 1941
106	ZN	Feb 1942
207	EM	Nov 1940

England, which could be laid accurately over any given target. A receiver in the aircraft enabled the pilot to locate the intersecting point and thus drop his bombs or markers exactly where they were required. A disadvantage of Oboe was that it could only be operated by one aircraft at a time, and this

Lancaster B.I 'IL-N' of No. 115 Sqn's 'C' Flight receives its lethal load at Witchford, Cambridgeshire in August 1944.

machine was required to fly an accurate track without any form of evasive action for ten minutes. In a slow bomber at comparatively low altitude, this was simply asking for trouble, but in an aircraft such as the Mosquito, which could operate at both high speed and altitude, the advantages far outweighed the disadvantages.

On 20/21 December 1942, six Mosquitoes of No. 109 Sqn. used Oboe for the first time in an attack on the power station at Lutterade. Three of the force successfully attacked the main target but the other three diverted to secondary targets when faults developed in their equipment. On New Year's Eve an Oboe-equipped Mosquito of No. 109 Sqn. marked Dusseldorf for Lancasters of No. 83 Sqn., dropping Skymarkers on the 10/10ths cloud which obscured the target. The heavies bombed on the markers but conditions prevented any accurate assessment of damage being made. The combination of Oboe and the Mosquito produced the perfect pathfinder to which the Germans had no effective answer, since the interception and shooting down of the de Havilland machine was a lot more difficult than the four-engined heavies. At this time, however, the Mosquito was not available in any quantity and pathfinder squadrons were using Stirlings, Halifaxes and Lancasters for marking purposes.

The other aid which was to be fitted to the main stream aircraft was H2S. This was an airborne radar set which displayed, on a screen, a 'picture' of the ground over which the aircraft was flying. It could therefore be used as a navigational aid and blind-bombing device, although in the latter role it was not too accurate as the received 'picture' was often ill-defined. The PFF was the first to use H2S, when Halifax and Stirling aircraft of Nos. 7 and 35 Sqns. led the Main Force against Hamburg on 30/31 January 1943. As more sets became available they were fitted to bombers operating in the main stream, but it was well into 1943 before all aircraft could be equipped. Being self-contained in the aircraft, H2S did not require any transmissions from ground stations and could not be jammed. Unfortunately, the Germans acquired a set from a Stirling soon after it was introduced to service. They were subsequently able to track aircraft using the device, both from ground stations and night fighters, which carried special tracking sets enabling them to home onto individual bombers.

The establishment of PFF and the introduction of Oboe and H2S combined to bring more satisfactory results at the end of 1942 and early 1943, enabling Harris and his planning staff to view the future with some optimism. In January 1943 Pathfinder Force was formed into its own group and from 8 January 1943, was No. 8 Group (PFF) with headquarters at Wyton. It eventually expanded from eight squadrons equipped with Stirlings, Wellingtons, Halifaxes and Lancasters in March 1943 to 19 squadrons equipped with Mosquitoes and Lancasters by the time the European war ended in 1945.

Another significant event which occurred in January 1943 was the Casablanca Conference, at which Churchill and Roosevelt together with their chiefs of staff discussed, among other items, the co-ordination of a combined bombing offensive. The conference was held in a mood of supreme optimism which appears to have inhibited the RAF contingent (which incidentally did not include Harris) from firmly pressing its views of mounting a full-scale strategic offensive against key industrial targets. Little consideration also appears to have been given to any plans the Germans might have been putting in hand to thwart any proposed offensive. Generals Spaatz and Eaker of the USAAF were present at this conference and made some outstanding claims as to what, in their opinion, a force of some 300 B-17 and B-24 bombers could do to German industry. Events proved that they had to learn their lesson the hard way, and it was not until early 1944 that the full weight of the American daylight raids began to have the telling effect forecast at Casablanca.[1]

1. This is an oversimplification of the discussions held, but those readers who wish to acquire a deeper insight into the Conference and indeed the whole subject of the strategic bomber offensive, can do so by referring to Anthony Verrier's informative study, *The Bomber Offensive* (B. T. Batsford Ltd. 1968 and Pan Books Ltd. 1974).

From the January deliberations came the famous Casablanca Directive, which was issued on the 21st and listed the following order of priorities for the Combined Bomber Offensive:

(1) German submarine construction yards.
(2) The German aircraft industry.
(3) Transportation.
(4) Oil plants.
(5) Other targets in enemy war industry.

Harris had on several occasions claimed that given a force of some 4,000 aircraft, Germany could be bombed into submission. Apart from the fact that the production of such a force was quite beyond realization, he was still regarded as something of a crank in certain quarters and his claims received little serious consideration. However, the carefully laid plans of Bomber Command to mount a full-scale offensive during 1943 went undisturbed, and the C-in-C realized that this would probably be his only chance of proving his point. Since he knew that all things being equal, the invasion of the European continent would go ahead in 1944—by which time American power would inevitably lead to a not

MOSQUITO SQUADRONS		
Squadron	*Code*	*First received*
21	YH	Sep 1943
45	OB	Feb 1944
82	UX	Jul 1944
84	VT	Feb 1945
105	GB	Nov 1941
107	OM	Feb 1944
109	HS	Dec 1942
110	VE	Nov 1944
128	M5	Sep 1944
139	XD	Nov 1942
142	4H	Oct 1944
162	CR	Dec 1944
163	?	Jan 1945
305	SM	Dec 1943
418	TH	Nov 1944
464	SB	Aug 1943
487	EG	Aug 1943
571	8K	Apr 1944
605	UP	Nov 1944
608	6T	Aug 1944
613	SY	Oct 1943
627	AZ	Nov 1943
692	P3	Jan 1944

Sergeant, later F/Off. James Henry Foy of No. 405 (Vancouver) Sqn. RCAF, tests his headset before embarking on a raid. Foy's shoulder flash is of interest since as a NCO he should have the RAF albatross under the 'CANADA' flash.

inconsequential amount of American control—it followed that his force would be required to attack and subdue tactical, rather than strategic targets. The operational inexperience of the USAAF bomber force in 1943 resulted in heavy losses during the daylight offensive and meant that the combined operations with Bomber Command were in the main confined only to paper directives. Throughout the year both air forces essentially went their separate ways.

The switch by the Luftwaffe to a defensive rather than offensive role and the reorganization of the night fighter force considerably affected the execution of the bomber offensive, with the result that in June 1943 the Casablanca Directive was modified in several respects, the most important of which was the priority destruction of the German fighter force—the Pointblank Directive. This intermediate directive was issued after some of the Casablanca aims had proved to be somewhat wishful thinking in the harsh reality of enemy airspace.

Having paid some lip-service to the original directive by attempting to bomb U-boat pens at St Nazaire and Lorient, Harris viewed his orders in the widest possible way and interpreted them accord-

ingly. His original task had been the destruction of German cities, which it was hoped would undermine morale and lessen the will to fight of the ordinary German citizen. The Casablanca Directive was aimed more towards industry, but Harris's views were stated quite openly in his book *Bomber Offensive*:

'. . . The subject of morale had been dropped, and I was now required to proceed with the general "disorganization" of German industry, giving priority to certain aspects of it such as U-boat building, aircraft production, oil production, transportation and so forth, which gave me a very wide range of choice and allowed me to attack pretty well any German industrial city of 100,000 inhabitants and above.'

The 'main offensive' as Harris was to call it in a post-war dispatch, can be broken down into three phases which have become known as the Battles of the Ruhr, Hamburg and Berlin. In each case the main concentration of attack was aimed repeatedly at the same target, the object being complete destruction. Other targets were, of course, attacked with a variety of forces, such raids being dictated by weather conditions, the need for decoys to divert enemy defences, their nuisance value, and tactical considerations.

The industrial area of the Ruhr was the first to receive Bomber Command's attention, with Essen being selected as the primary target on the night of 5/6 March. Mosquitoes of the PFF dropped red target indicators at 20.58hrs, followed by green markers from 22 four-engined heavies. The first wave of Main Force comprised 69 Halifaxes of Nos. 1, 4 and 6 Groups, with 52 Stirlings and 131 Wellingtons in the second wave. These two waves dropped their combined high explosives (HEs) and incendiaries accurately on the red markers, which had been dropped with the aid of Oboe, starting extensive fires to guide the third formation of 140 Lancasters to deposit their HEs accurately into the blazing inferno.

The execution of the Essen raid was typical of the methods to be used throughout 1943: the policy of concentrating a large proportion of high explosive bombs in the final wave being to disrupt the fire-fighting and rescue services. Over 600 acres of Essen were destroyed and large areas of the Krupps works were laid to waste at a total cost of fourteen bombers. This represented a loss rate of just over 3 per cent, which was 50 per cent below the loss rate the command estimated it could sustain for a concentrated series of raids over a three month period.

The attack on Essen proved that Oboe was the answer to accurate target location as the intersecting beams placed precisely over the aiming point enabled marking to be carried out effectively even when the target was obscured by cloud, smoke, industrial haze or a combination of all three. German night fighters were hard pushed to make any form of impression on the Oboe Mosquitoes, so the disadvantage of flying straight and level during the 'homing' and marking was minimized. There were other disadvantages however, the most acute being the range at which Oboe could be used effectively. Beyond Oboe range, H2S had to be used for location and marking purposes which introduced a greater degree of 'human element', as the equipment was completely self-contained in the aircraft and gave, by modern standards, a very primitive form of ground display. H2S could be used to distinguish general land masses and city areas and prevented a certain amount of wastage by the scattering of bombs over open land, but it did not give the same concentration as Oboe. This was graphically proved on the night of 8/9 March when Nuremberg was the target for 335 aircraft. The city was marked by Nos. 7 and 35 Sqns., which dropped their red target indicators blind by H2S. The TIs were scattered over a wide area and the subsequent green flares dropped by the backers-up gave Main Force a wide choice of aiming points. Although the damage created certainly caused problems in the medieval city, and the MAN factory, Sieman Schukert works and other industrial installations received their fair share of attention, the devastation was not nearly as concentrated as it had been in Essen.

The average strength of a Main Force during the forty-three major raids which constituted the Battle of the Ruhr between March and July was between 300 and 700 aircraft, the highest total being 826 which attacked Dortmund on 23 May. Although most of these raids were centred on nine major targets within the Ruhr, many other smaller targets both inside 'Happy Valley' (as it became known by the crews) and further afield in Germany were attacked. This diversification prevented the defenders from concentrating all their resources

Pleasing air-to-air photograph of an early Lancaster B.I without the dorsal turret fairing, on the strength of No. 83 Sqn.

within a known area of attack, as well as keeping them guessing as to where the main thrust was to come. The planned route to the target was made known to crews at briefing, but at various points along it smaller forces which had operated with the main stream up to that particular point would break off on a 'spoof' raid.

On the ground the German radar controllers could tell that a raid was developing but as traces began to divert they found it difficult to decide exactly where the Main Force was heading. Naturally, skills on both sides developed, and some ground controllers developed a knack of interpreting the potential target quicker than others, in what can only be termed a lethal cat-and-mouse game. Those who were able to vector their night fighters into the bomber stream accurately achieved a tremendous feeling of self-satisfaction, but once they had done their job, the onus lay with the night fighter pilot and his radar operator, who could only hope that their skills exceeded those of their quarry.

THE CREWS

Concurrent with the 1943 offensive the German ground and air defences were greatly increased and improved to meet the threat the German High Command knew must come. This aspect of the air war is one which does not appear to have had the consideration it should have done at Casablanca. The increased use of ground-controlled radar, as well as interception radar installed in night fighters, had a tremendous effect on the efficiency of the squadrons which would now defend their homeland with the same enthusiasm as their RAF counterparts had done in 1940–1942. Backing this force was a vast number of searchlights, many of which were radar controlled, as well as a chain of anti-aircraft guns ranging from 88mm to 137mm in calibre. These guns were concentrated in areas of intense RAF activity and like the searchlights, many of them were controlled by radar predictors. Anti-aircraft guns were an expensive form of defence as

Among a number of aircraft types that were unable to prove themselves in the unforgiving skies of Europe, yet do well in other theatres, was the Lockheed Ventura. After a short career with three squadrons in No. 2 Group it was replaced by Mosquitoes.

At this point the alertness of the bomber's gunners, the co-operation between the whole crew, and to a certain degree luck, was all that stood between survival to return another day, and death or a PoW camp.

far as quantity of ammunition was concerned; up to 31 December 1942 an average of 4,057 rounds had been required for every aircraft shot down and by the end of 1944 this figure had risen to 33,500.

Bomber crews were routed to avoid known areas of anti-aircraft batteries and searchlights, but since most selected targets were ringed by such defences, there inevitably came a period on every operation when they had to be faced. The cover of darkness and weaving during the approach and exit to the

A trio of Lancasters of No. 44 Sqn. photographed from a fourth aircraft. KM-Y and KM-W have dorsal turret fairings although KM-S in the background does not. (Hawker Siddeley)

target afforded the bombers some protection against flak, but basically there was no defence since the approach of shells could not be seen, and a concentrated barrage into the area of the main stream was almost certain to claim some victims. A near miss could throw a bomber into the path of one of its companions, whilst a hit on some part of the aircraft's structure could lead to its destruction or cripple it to an extent where it dropped from the protection of the main stream and became an easier victim for prowling night-fighters. So although the cost in ammunition per aircraft actually destroyed by guns was high, near misses and damaging hits could also lead to the eventual loss of the bomber, either to night fighters, or by crash damage when it eventually returned to its home base.

Direct hits in the area of the bomb-bay or fuel tanks were invariably fatal and on such occasions the crew probably never knew what had hit them, so survival, even by parachute, was extremely remote. Bomber crews used the chest type parachute which had to be clipped onto the harness when the decision to abandon the aircraft was taken. The packs were stored in the aircraft in convenient positions near each crew station and it can be appreciated that if the aircraft received a flak hit which caused it to disintegrate, men could be thrown out without their parachutes. Rear gunners, who probably had the most dangerous position, stored their 'chutes' in the aircraft's fuselage near the turret doors. If the order to abandon the aircraft came, they had to swivel their turret so that the doors lined up with the fuselage, retrieve their parachute, and clip it on; then get out, through the fuselage hatch, or by swinging the turret at right angles to the aircraft's centre-line and making a backward somersault through the turret doors.

In some later marks of the Lancaster the four Browning Frazer-Nash rear turret was replaced by a roomier Rose-Rice turret which carried two 0·05in machine guns. The latter enabled the gunner to wear a pilot-type parachute in which the pack was attached to the harness and formed a cushion on which he sat. One particular ex-gunner who owes his life to this arrangement is Sergeant R. McCann. On Christmas Eve 1944 McCann's Lancaster was attacking Cologne, the tenth trip for the ninteeen year old gunner, who now freely admits that he was terrified during every minute of all of them, despite never having once seen a night fighter or fired his guns in anger. McCann remembers hearing the bomb-aimer intoning 'left . . . left . . . left . . . steady . . . steady . . .' to the captain, then a tremendous explosion. He recovered consciousness swinging under his parachute canopy from which he was suspended by the ankles, with the fires of Cologne revolving below him. He managed to scramble into an upright position before hitting the ground in a field adjacent to an anti-aircraft battery, the crew of which had not seen his descent. The shock of one moment being seemingly safe in his aircraft, and the next on the ground in enemy territory can be summed up in his own words:

'I just didn't realize what had happened and my actions in hiding my parachute and burying other equipment were purely automatic. I then wondered what I should do but before I could make any positive decision my emotions overcame me and I sat down, lit a cigarette and cried for my family who had in fact presented me with the cigarette case I had just used, when I received my air gunner's brevet.'

McCann eventually crawled away from the site of the anti-aircraft battery but was soon captured and after treatment at a local hospital was transferred to PoW camp where he spent the rest of the war.[1]

It is likely that McCann's Lancaster suffered a direct hit in its bomb-bay, or the 4,000lb bomb it was carrying was struck just after leaving the aircraft, a fate which probably accounted for many bombers and one over which the crew had no control. His comments about the emotional strain are interesting in that this theme is often echoed by surviving bomber crews. An infantryman moving into the front line, or a sailor on board a ship on convoy duty, knew that death or injury was lurking around every corner for twenty-four hours a day; bomber crew members faced a constant mental adjustment to accept such facts. During their operational tour of thirty trips, they lived in comparatively peaceful surroundings, enjoyed trips to the 'local' with their friends, leave with their

1. Recounted in an interview with the author.

LANCASTER SQUADRONS		
Squadron	*Code*	*First received*
7	MG	July 1943
9	WS	Aug 1942
12	PH	Nov 1942
15	LS	Dec 1943
35	TL	Mar 1944
44	KM	Dec 1941
49	EA	June 1942
50	VN	May 1942
57	DX	Sept 1942
61	QR	Apr 1942
75	AA	Mar 1944
83	OL	May 1942
90	WP	May 1944
97	OF	Jan 1942
100	HW	Jan 1943
101	SR	Oct 1942
103	PM	Oct 1942
106	ZN	May 1942
115	KO/A4/IL	Mar 1944
138	AC/NF	Mar 1945
149	OJ	Aug 1944
150	IQ	Nov 1944
153	P4	Oct 1944
156	GT	Jan 1943
166	AS	Sept 1943
170	TC	Oct 1944
186	XY/AP	Oct 1944
189	CA	Oct 1944
195	AC/JE	Oct 1944
207	EM	Mar 1942
218	HA	Aug 1944
227	9J	Oct 1944
300	BH	Apr 1944
405	LQ	Aug 1943
424	QB	Jan 1945
427	ZL	Mar 1945
428	NA	Jun 1944
429	AL	Mar 1945
431	SE	Oct 1944
432	QO	Oct 1943
433	BM	Jan 1945
434	IP	Dec 1944
460	AR	Oct 1942
463	PO/JO	Nov 1943
467	PO	Nov 1942
514	J1/A2	Jun 1944
550	BQ	Nov 1943
576	UL	Nov 1943
582	6O	Apr 1944
617	AJ/KC/YZ	Mar 1943
619	PG	Apr 1943
622	GI	Dec 1943
625	CF	Oct 1943
626	UM	Nov 1943
630	LE	Nov 1943
635	F2	Mar 1944

A Halifax B.II Series 1a of No. 78 Sqn. in its element above the clouds. The series 1a retained the Merlin engines of the Mk.II but was fitted with rectangular fins/rudders during 1943 to cure the rudder stalling experienced with the original triangular fins.

families, and the normal social life prevalent on RAF stations; but when a raid was announced they had a few hours to adjust themselves to the holocaust they would face during the forthcoming trip, the time over the target, and the return. First came an air test in which they would try their equipment, then a wait while the pilots and navigators attended their briefing, then another wait before the main briefing at which they would be made aware of their target, then yet more waiting until time for take-off. During these periods of waiting, each man would pass the time in a way suitable to his own temperament. Some would fiddle with their aircraft and its equipment, others would rest quietly in their rooms maybe writing letters, whilst the more extrovert, who in many cases were the most nervous, would attempt to hide their nervousness by playing boisterous games of soccer, rugby or cricket. As take-off time approached they would draw their parachutes from stores, often cracking the old familiar joke with the WAAF packers 'If it doesn't work, love, I shall bring it back'; escape rations were checked over and over again, then finally came the ride in the crew bus to their aircraft parked at dispersal.

Before boarding the aircraft, there would be a final cigarette or two, jokes would be told, and in many cases, set superstitious rituals would be followed. Lady Luck was appeased in many ways, one of the most usual being for the whole crew to relieve themselves over the aircraft's tail wheel before boarding, which sometimes followed a set sequence, the breaking of which was almost certain to tempt fate. Once aboard with mascots stowed in familiar places, and the job of getting the aircraft started and each crew member checking and verifying the serviceability of his equipment under way, tension drained away as training and team spirit took over.

On the return, debriefing was followed by a meal, maybe a linger around flying control for news of missing comrades, then perhaps a restless sleep before the dawn of another day which might or might not bring another operation. The cold light of the new day would bring moments of poignant memory as familiar faces were missed in the mess and the personal belongings of those who had 'bought it' were packed to be returned to their next-

With the briefing behind them Lancaster crews share a joke with an administration officer before going to their aircraft. Again a variety of uniform and flying kit is in evidence.

of-kin; but soon new faces with shining stripes and brevets would appear, and those left, some of whom might only have completed one of their scheduled 30 trips, would become veterans and the whole cycle would repeat.

The situation facing bomber crews with their daily flirtation with normality and the 'Grim Reaper' is graphically illustrated by Flying Officer Patrick Hemming, a navigator who completed his tour with No. 15 Sqn. on Lancasters. He wrote:

I am very bitter when modern day books describe the bomber as a sitting target. I feel that this is unjustified, as on my squadron fighters were claimed by air gunners on nearly every sortie, and these were not made lightly. Indeed, bomber crews were not given enough credit even by Harris himself. Prior to D-Day Harris did not consider

The rear gunner of a Halifax checks the ammunition feeds to his turret.

his crews accurate enough for operations other than area bombing.

In my opinion this was not the case, although I can only speak of my squadron which was then equipped with all the modern equipment such as H2S, Gee and G-H. Post D-Day he seemed to have been converted to tactical bombing and his crews were given the chance to show their skills.

It is my own firm conviction that if he had concentrated on targets such as oil refineries, communications and transport systems, rather than cities, Germany would have been brought to her knees much sooner.

To put into words the emotions of the job I did is not easy, indeed to the generation of today, the thought exists as to whether or not it was worth it. I think it was, and am convinced that world history would differ enormously had the Germans emerged as victors.

I don't think I was ever really afraid, except perhaps for my first raid, the symptoms of that being universal. The body seems to have an inbuilt safety valve and as you progressed into your tour, the fear of death became remote; even death itself seemed unreal. The only emotions you really felt were when you walked into the dining room and saw the empty chairs and thought to

yourself 'It looks as though old so-and-so has finally bought it'.

Today's generation have never had to face life in this its most bitterest form, which makes their scepticism so understandable. The only time I felt real emotion was the death of a fellow navigator whose Lancaster was hit by a 4,000lb bomb dropped by a higher flying Halifax. For a while I was very depressed; it would have been different somehow if it had been a night fighter or Flak. The Halifax never did have a place in my affections after that. I was also saddened by the odd occasion when the strain proved too much, and remember when one Canadian pilot during his second tour cracked up and dived his aircraft at the target calling the Germans all the adjectives under the sun and making clear his intentions of placing the Lancaster and its load firmly on to the aiming point. The flight engineer managed to overpower him and flew the aircraft back to base where he crash-landed it. The whole crew survived and happily the pilot, after treatment, went to an OCU.

The reality of survival increased with each trip but sometimes security was shattered at the eleventh hour. I

The all-NCO crew of a No. 2 Group Boston squadron discuss a forthcoming low-level raid over occupied Europe.

well remember one of our crews who had completed 29 ops being given an easy target for their last. This was the port of Le Havre. After sweeping over the target and doing their half-minute's work they turned for home and their feelings must have been over-jubilant for they dropped their guard and were shot down by a night fighter. There were no survivors and [theirs was] the only aircraft lost that night.

By mid-1943 both the aircraft and crews Harris needed were becoming available in greater quantity. The aircraft, mainly Lancasters and Halifaxes, would never reach the operational figure of 4,000 that the C-in-C had once claimed would win the war in one campaign, but there were now over 800 available to operate in strength on big raids. The Empire Air Training Programme, with flying schools established in Canada, America, Rhodesia, Australia and South Africa, was producing crews in sufficient numbers to man the aircraft as well as replace those whose tours had ended. The men now manning bombers came from every country and walk of life. Canada's contribution was considerable, over 22,000 aircrew being trained in Canadian schools from mid-1942 to the war's end, No. 6 Group becoming operational from 1 January 1943 as No. 6 (RCAF) Group. Men from Australia, New Zealand, France, Poland, Czechoslovakia and a host of other countries, including America, from whence some men paid their own passages to enlist in the RAF before their own country entered the war, answered the call and joined the ranks of Bomber Command. A considerable number gave their lives alongside their British colleagues before hostilities ended, at which time 55,573 aircrew had died on active service.

During 1943 the life expectancy of a crew was just under eleven operations at its best, and just over

The ground crews or 'erks' were just as important to Bomber Command as aircrew. Here, engine fitters, armourers and instrument mechanics attend to Lancaster B.I L7540 of No. 83 Sqn., an aircraft that also served with Nos. 44 and 207 Sqns. and several operational conversion units before being struck-off-charge in April 1944.

eight on average, as the pendulum swung to and fro between the attackers and the defenders. After initial training crews teamed up at Operational Conversion Units, where the bond of friendship could turn into the essential ingredient of interdependent teamwork, a valuable asset in the survival stakes once operations started.

In the RAF, the captain of the aircraft, irrespective of rank, was the pilot. It was his leadership and guidance that went a long way to moulding the six others who formed the team into an efficient fighting force. Constant practice and self-criticism of everything from dinghy drill to the maintenance of equipment, helped to strengthen the weakest link in the chain, and ensure that it would not break under duress. Those crews who took every aspect of their training seriously, both official and self-imposed, stood a far higher chance of survival than those who perhaps preferred another drink at the local or a game of cards to a few more minutes on the range, in the W/T cabin or the Link trainer, or the study of enemy aircraft silhouettes.

As the German night fighter crews became more proficient, gunners had to keep a constant vigil, ready to shout a warning to their pilots—a warning that had to be responded to quickly and without question. Gunners who carried out their lonely vigils from the tail turrets frequently removed the perspex centre-panels between their four Brownings, to give them an unobstructed view of the hostile sky. This resulted in a drafty cold ride, but as Sgt. K. Wood, a gunner from No. 149 Sqn. said: 'It was better to be cold and alive, than dead cold!' Sergeant Wood completed his tour with the rank of F/Off. and had one Bf110 to his credit; his captain always acted promptly on his instructions and on one occasion this resulted in the crew having a very rough ride for a five minute period.

After bombing Dusseldorf and leaving the target area without incident, the crew started to relax as the Lancaster headed home. Some twenty minutes later, the ever vigilant Sgt. Wood saw a night fighter with its landing light on approaching the aircraft; without giving any thought to this unusual occurrence he immediately ordered the pilot to corkscrew starboard. This manoeuvre, in which the aircraft was thrown into a spiralling dive then pulled up

continued on page 33

Flight Lieutenant, Royal Australian Air Force, 1944, wearing standard service dress uniform in distinctive Australian dark blue. Gilt albatross badge above cuff ranking was also a national peculiarity, of same design as forage cap badge. Beneath pilot's brevet on left breast he wears ribbons of Distinguished Flying Cross and Air Force Cross.

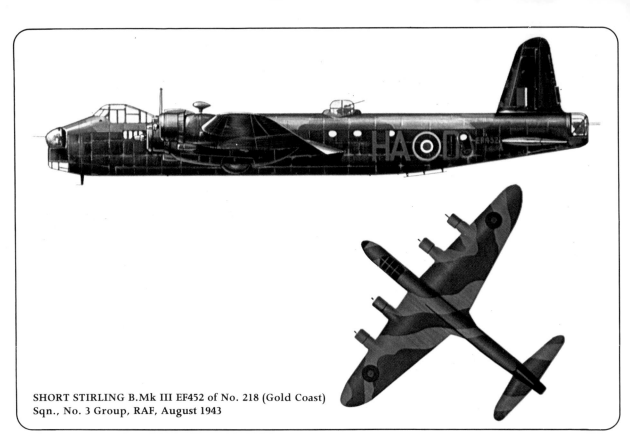

SHORT STIRLING B.Mk III EF452 of No. 218 (Gold Coast)
Sqn., No. 3 Group, RAF, August 1943

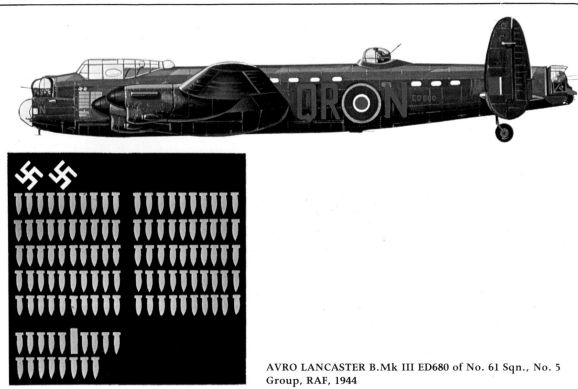

AVRO LANCASTER B.Mk III ED680 of No. 61 Sqn., No. 5
Group, RAF, 1944

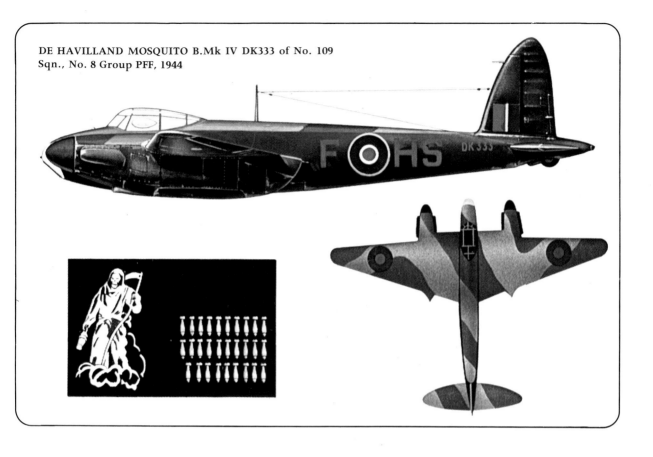

DE HAVILLAND MOSQUITO B.Mk IV DK333 of No. 109 Sqn., No. 8 Group PFF, 1944

DK 333

OPPOSITE TOP: **Short Stirling B.Mk III EF452 of No. 218 (Gold Coast) Sqn., No. 3 Group, Downham Market, Suffolk, August 1943.** This aircraft was flown by F/Sgt. A. Aaron on the night of 12/13 August, a sortie to Turin which resulted in the second Victoria Cross to go to a Stirling captain. The machine bears Dark Earth/Dark Green camouflage pattern 4 on the upper surfaces, with Night Black undersides, fuselage roundels being 54in diameter Type C1, wing roundels 75in diameter Type B. Code letters were 4ft high on the Stirling, with the 8in high serial taking up 29in. Aaron's crew for the Turin raid was: Sgt. W. Brennan (Navigator), F/Sgt. A. Larden (Bomb Aimer), and Sgts. J. Guy (W/Op), M. Mitchem (F/Eng), Richmond (Mid-upper Gunner) and McCabe (Rear Gunner).

OPPOSITE BOTTOM: **Avro Lancaster B.Mk III ED680 of No. 61 Sqn., No. 5 Group, Skellingthorpe, Lincs, 1944.** Depicted as it appeared after 118 operational sorties, this Lancaster was written off in a take-off accident on the night of 28/29 October 1944 when setting out for a raid on Bergen. Its 100th trip was made on 27/28 June 1944, a sortie to Vitry-La-François with F/Lt. B. Turner at the controls, the machine having joined No. 61 Sqn. in August 1943 after serving with No. 156 since April 1943. In standard Bomber Command camouflage, the aircraft's sortie record was presented as rows of ten bomb symbols, the 106th sortie being indicated by the silhouette of a 4,000lb 'Cookie', and two enemy aircraft destroyed by accompanying swastikas. Fuselage roundels were 54in diameter Type C1, those on the wings 95in diameter Type B; the serial was 8in high and 29in long.

ABOVE: **De Havilland Mosquito B.Mk IV DK333 of No. 109 Sqn., No. 8 Group PFF, Wyton, Hunts, 1944.** Painted in standard day bomber camouflage of Dark Green and Ocean Grey on the upper surfaces with Night Black undersides, the aircraft is depicted after completion of twenty-nine operations. As with heavy bombers, Mosquitoes often sported distinctive 'nose art' adjacent to their operational record, the figure of the 'Grim Reaper' being all too appropriate to the bomber offensive. Fuselage roundels on Mosquitoes were 36in diameter Type C1, with 54in diameter Type B on the wings.

BISHOP'S BASHER

HANDLEY PAGE HALIFAX B.Mk II Srs Ia HR946, No. 51 Sqn., No. 4 Group, November 1943

PAGES 28–29: Handley Page Halifax B.Mk II Series Ia HR946, No. 51 Sqn., No. 4 Group, Snaith, Yorkshire, November 1943. Issued to No. 51 Sqn. in July 1943, HR946 remained with that unit until January 1944 when it was transferred to No. 77 Sqn. at Elvington to become KN-X. Finished in standard Dark Earth/Dark Green/Night Black camouflage, the aircraft had 54in diameter Type C1 fuselage roundels and 95in diameter Type B wing roundels, 4ft high code letters and 8in high serials. The artwork shows the Halifax as of the afternoon of 10 November 1943 just prior to its fifteenth trip, a sortie to Cannes that night. The crew on that operation (the last with this particular crew) was: Plt. Off. T. Bishop (Pilot), Plt. Off. J. Neve (Navigator), Plt. Off. K. Isaacs (Bomb Aimer), Plt. Off. J. Boulter (W/Op), and Sgts. Wales (Flight Engineer), Holder (Mid-upper Gunner) and Waldon (Rear Gunner). A 15th bomb silhouette was added to the log on the afternoon of 11 November, the crew having dropped poppies over France on their way back from Cannes in an unofficial gesture to the French people to mark Remembrance Day.

BELOW: Handley Page Halifax B.Mk VII NP763 of No. 346 'Guyenne' Squadron, French Air Force, No. 4 Group, Elvington, Yorks, 1944–45. One of two Halifax squadrons manned by French personnel, No. 346's machines had their fuselage roundels 'reversed' in the sequence of French national markings and carried the distinctive tail markings applied by a number of squadrons in No. 4 Group RAF for identification purposes on daylight operations. This aircraft also exhibits yellow-outlined code letters, with the individual aircraft letter repeated on the fins in line with widespread practice of the period.

OPPOSITE TOP: A selection of insignia and markings. (A) Personal marking of Halifax B.Mk III LV860/KW-U of No. 425 Sqn. RCAF. (B) Personal marking of Lancaster B.III PB532/HW-S², No. 100 Sqn., April 1945. The name stemmed from the South American origins of the pilot, Flt. Lt. O. Lloyd-Davies and the 'squared' individual aircraft letter is shown, together with a 'noteworthy' operational record! (C) Insignia sported by a number of No. 105 Sqn. Mosquitoes. (D) Tail marking of Lancaster B.III of No. 97 (Straits Settlements) Sqn., August 1944. (E) Markings denoting a G-H leader's Lancaster. (F) Tail marking, Halifax B.VI, No. 102 Sqn. (G) Tail marking, Halifax B.III, No. 462 Sqn. RAAF. (H) Examples of bomber markings used to record operations flown and decorations won—in this case the DFC (white/purple) and DSO (red/blue). (I) Chalked marking, Halifax B.III MZ714/KW-Y, No. 425 Sqn. RCAF—third row of 25 bomb symbols not shown.

OPPOSITE BOTTOM: Bomber Command Austin K2 ambulance with wing marking indicating a vehicle used by No. 3 Group and a typical registration plate.

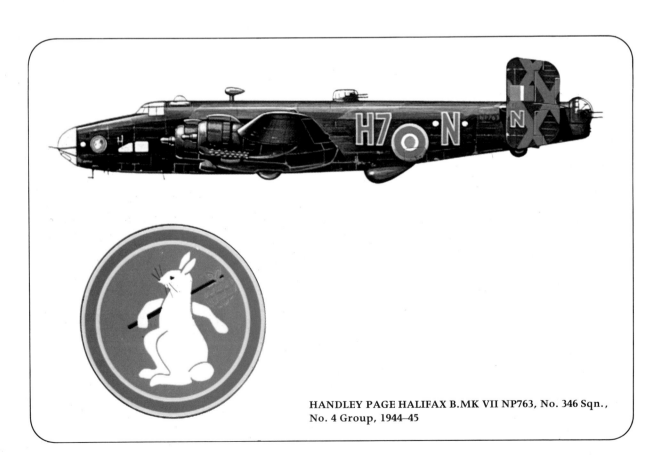

HANDLEY PAGE HALIFAX B.MK VII NP763, No. 346 Sqn., No. 4 Group, 1944–45

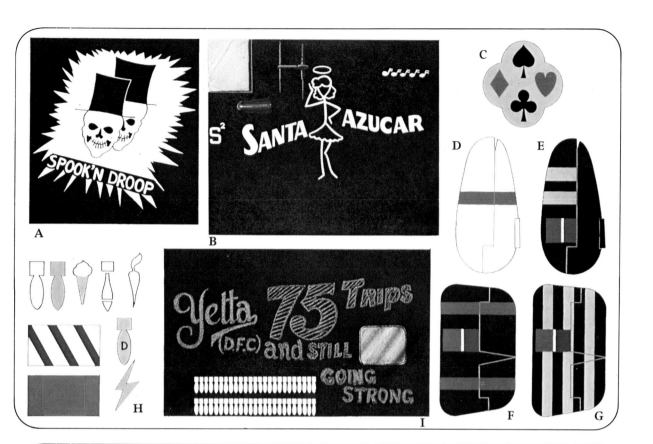

AUSTIN K2 ambulance used by No. 3 Group Bomber Command

Flight Sergeant of a Polish squadron, 1943–44, in service dress with mixture of RAF and Polish Air Force insignia: RAF other ranks' cap badge; RAF other ranks albatross shoulder patch with 'POLAND' above motif; Polish button above RAF chevrons; and Polish rank collar patches of gold lace on RAF blue.

Air Gunner, 1944, in complete flying clothing with late Type C wired flying helmet. The sheepskin Irvin jacket and matching trousers are worn, with 'escape' type boots: the suede legs could be removed in emergency, the feet resembling civilian shoes. The parachute harness is worn over the uninflated life jacket, and a parachute pack is carried.

into a climbing turn in the opposite direction, was accomplished, but still the night fighter hung grimly in the same position. Sergeant Wood again told his skipper and the Lancaster once more lurched into a stomach-dragging corkscrew, this time to port.

When the Lancaster straightened up, the fighter was still holding its position. Sergeant Wood then decided to allow it to close in before advising any more evasive action, and for the next three minutes, which he says seemed like three centuries, the light still hovered behind the Lancaster. At last the embarrassed sergeant realized that he had been telling his captain to take avoiding action against a star! Although there was some light-hearted ribbing from his colleagues, there was no criticism, and the incident was not mentioned again until their tour was over.

Another gunner who pleaded with his skipper to let him have a go at an Me410 which was flying below his aircraft, was the rear gunner of Fg. Off. Hemming's No. 15 Sqn. Lancaster. The preamble to this unusual request occurred on the crew's first operation to Dreux on 10 June 1944. After bombing the target, the aircraft was attacked by a Bf109 which stuck with it through the standard corkscrew evasive action. As the Lancaster pulled out of its third corkscrew, the enemy pilot misjudged his speed and fell away under the bomber, exposing his aircraft's belly to the rear gunner. An accurate burst from the four ·303in machine guns hit the 109's belly tank, which immediately exploded. The sudden flash in the sky attracted the attention of a Ju88 which bore in from the port quarter. The gunner called 'Fighter port quarter, corkscrew starboard'. Not having heard the last instruction, the captain queried which way, and in unison the crew bawled into their intercoms 'Bloody starboard!' The Ju88 stayed with the Lancaster, making eight attacks before it broke off the engagement over the Channel. During this time the bomber was hit several times and the violent manoeuvres had thrown all navigational equipment into complete disarray. Flying Officer Hemmings navigated home with the aid of a piece of string and a book acting as a straight edge. The gunner was credited with the Bf109 and received much publicity in his home town during which the mayor agreed to present him

RAF firemen wearing protective asbestos suits for fighting aircraft fires or carrying out rescues. The fireman on the right is holding a foam spray.

with £10 if he could shoot down another night fighter. Three trips later a lone Me410 appeared below the Lancaster—which the German pilot had obviously not seen—and the impecunious gunner pleaded with the skipper. However the latter would not grant the plaintive requests, deciding—quite rightly—that there was nothing to be gained from advertising his aircraft's position. For the remainder of the crew's tour no other night fighters were encountered so the gunner was denied his £10 reward. Stories such as this serve to outline the importance of strong crew discipline; a less conscientious gunner might well have opened fire on the Me410, failed to hit it and as a result jeopardized the whole crew, for a well-flown Me410 was more than a match for the machine gun armament of a Lancaster.

FIRE STORM

The opening raids in the Battle of the Ruhr proved the value of Oboe and to a lesser degree H2S, which was handicapped at this stage by a relatively low serviceability rate—about 45 per cent of sets being out of action by the time the target was reached—and the inferior performance, when compared with the Oboe-carrying Mosquitoes, of the four-engined heavies in which it was installed. Many of these latter were Stirlings, which suffered from a severe lack of speed and ability to operate at altitudes above 12,000ft. Nonetheless results were beginning to tell and the Main Force was able to make more bombs count than it had before the advent of target and route marking. The latter was another function of PFF and proved particularly valuable when encountered winds turned out to be different from those forecast. The meteorology officers did a good job under difficult circumstances, but denied vital information over the Continent, they had to rely a great deal on calculated estimations. At briefing all navigators were informed of likely weather conditions and winds they would encounter en route. Variations in wind direction and speed could quickly alter the planned track so it was vital that any changes were passed to the Main Force as

Although not having to face the hazards the aircrew did, groundcrew did not always have a happy lot. In winter time at dispersal, which could be several miles from their normal accommodation, airmen would show their skills of improvisation by building temporary shelters from practically anything they could beg, borrow or steal.

Lancaster office. Close-up of the controls of the mainstay of Bomber Command after 1942 showing the pilot's control column and engine throttle quadrant.

quickly as possible. To do this, PFF aircraft and the lead formations would broadcast winds to those behind, thus enabling navigators to make the necessary changes to their calculations. It must be remembered that although the bombers flew in close proximity to each other, every navigator was responsible for the course of his individual aircraft; there was no question of a master navigator leading the whole stream. Bomber operations on three consecutive nights were unusual, but between 26–29 March Duisburg, St Nazaire and Berlin were attacked, the latter by a force of 329 while another 150 aircraft carried out a diversionary raid on Bochum. The defences of the German capital were particularly formidable and it took great courage to

Lancaster B.I 'WS-V' of No. 9 Sqn. This aircraft was flown by F/Off. J. Cowan, who christened all his aircraft 'Barbara-Mary'. This pilot's Wellington carrying the same name is illustrated in *RAF Bomber Units 1939–42*. (R. Leask-Ward)

Nose art of a Halifax Mk.III, with the Vickers Gas Operated gun (VGO) clearly visible in the nose transparency. (via R. Leask-Ward)

face the many radar-controlled searchlights and anti-aircraft guns which surrounded the city. Defences such as those at Berlin led to a bombing phenomenon known as 'creep back', which occurred as crews released their loads early. It only needed an early attacker to release his bombs short of the aiming point for others to drop on his fires, then another to drop short of these and so on, to magnify the error quite considerably by the time the last aircraft in the stream bombed. This problem was never satisfactorily solved, but the fitting of cameras which recorded the release point, and remarking by Backers-up if they saw the original markers being obliterated, helped to cure it. The introduction of a Master Bomber, who directed the whole attack by VHF radio, over which he could call on new markers, tell the main stream to ignore spoof

were breached but eight of the Lancasters failed to return, representing a loss rate of 42 per cent, which was clearly unacceptable for a series of sustained attacks of a similar nature.

By 14 July the Battle of the Ruhr was over. The forty-three major raids had cost Bomber Command 872 aircraft, a loss rate of 4·7 per cent, which was just below the estimated rate the command could sustain. Photographic evidence indicated that considerable damage had been caused, but post-war records prove that this had not upset production as much as was thought at the time. This in no way detracts from the efforts made by the gallant crews, since it must be remembered that one of the major aims was to upset civilian morale. This had been achieved to a degree and was to be considerably increased by the next series of raids which became

No. 83 Sqn. Lancasters line up ready for the start of another raid.

fires or poor markers, and generally act as a 'master of ceremonies', was a great step forward in bombing techniques.

The origination of the Master Bomber can be traced to the famous Dams raid by No. 617 Sqn. on the night of 16/17 May. This raid, led by Wg. Cdr. Guy Gibson, came during the Battle of the Ruhr, and was a deviation from the planned area bombing offensive, being a precision attack on what was considered to be a vital target. The squadron was formed specifically to perform this task, for which it used specially developed bouncing mines designed by Dr. Barnes Wallis. The nineteen Lancasters flew at low level over their targets and released their mines at a set speed and altitude. After making his attack, Gibson directed the other Lancasters and drew enemy defensive fire away from each aircraft as it made its bomb run. The Möhne and Eder Dams

known as the Battle of Hamburg.

The first raids were to be significant, for they saw the first use of a simple radar-jamming device, and brought in their wake the terror of the 'firestorm'. For some time scientists had been working on a method of jamming German ground radar, and had in fact come up with a very simple and inexpensive counter-measure which they christened 'Window'. Consisting of strips of aluminium foil, each one measuring 30 centimetres long and 1·5 centimetres wide, Window was dropped in bundles of 2,000 strips held together by an elastic band. As each bundle was released it formed a cloud of aluminium strips which gave an echo on radar the same size as that received from a bomber. Released at one minute intervals from every bomber in the

Wing Commander C. Hopcroft's Lancaster B.III ED707 'Frederick II'. All this pilot's aircraft were called Frederick after the code letter 'F', Frederick III being ED989. Wing Commander Hopcroft was the CO of No. 57 Sqn. (via R. Leask-Ward)

force, Window saturated enemy radar screens to such an extent that controlled interceptions became impossible. This simple device had been perfected in 1942, but its use by Bomber Command was prohibited until such time as British radar immune to such jamming had been developed, since it was believed that the Germans would soon realize the effectiveness of it and use it themselves. Unknown to the British, German scientists had developed the same type of jamming method in parallel, and had not used it for the very same reason! Such are the exigencies of war.

By July 1943 Bomber Command had expanded into a striking force beyond all recognition of what it had been, whilst the Luftwaffe bomber force had been reduced to almost total impotence. The time was now right to try Window in an endeavour to cut the increasing losses to night fighters.

On the night of 24/25 July 1943, a force of 791

bombers set course for Hamburg, which was beyond the range of Oboe and so was to be marked by PFF aircraft using H2S. Being situated on a river and close to the sea, Hamburg presented an ideal target for H2S marking as its characteristic almost guaranteed a good 'picture'. As the leading aircraft passed over Heligoland, they started releasing their bundles of Window; the effect was immediate, and the German defences were thrown into total confusion. The first aircraft to reach Hamburg were 110 Lancasters from Nos. 1 and 5 Groups, and their crews were immediately struck by the total absence of night fighters, and the way the radar-controlled searchlights seemed to wander aimlessly around the sky. The Primary Markers had accurately marked the target using H2S and these indicators were soon followed by the reds of the Visual Markers and the greens of the Backers-up. The Main Force had little problem in depositing their various loads of 8,000lb, 4,000lb, 1,000lb and canisters of 4lb incendiaries on the markers, and Hamburg was soon a raging inferno. July had been a particularly dry month, resulting in ideal conditions for a concentrated incendiary attack; as the fires increased in intensity, the air above them was heated causing it to rise. As it did so, more air rushed in to take its place and created winds which fanned the flames. This air also became heated and the process became a self-repeating cycle. Small fires were fanned into big conflagrations and the hurricane-force winds created spread the inferno until an area of over nine miles square was blazing.

Returning crews reported that they could see the fires of Hamburg from as far away as 100 miles, and they knew that this was only the overture, since Harris had warned them that Hamburg would not be destroyed in one night. The loss of 12 aircraft (1·5 per cent) proved to the crews that Window did all that was claimed, and those who regarded the dropping of it as another chore, very quickly changed their opinions.

The American 8th Air Force visited the city on the following two days, and small forces of Mosquitoes carried out nuisance raids before the next major assault on the night of 27/28 July. This time 787 aircraft took part and, again in ideal conditions, started many new fires which created an even bigger fire-storm, causing a cloud of smoke to rise to over 20,000 feet and form a sinister shroud over the doomed city. This time 17 aircraft (2·13 per cent) failed to return but by previous loss rates this

was well within the accepted parameters.

The third raid on Hamburg came on the night of 29/30 July when 777 bombers revisited the scene of devastation, their navigators needing very little outside aid to find the target which by now was a seething mass of flames. On this occasion the night fighter force used new tactics, their crews operating on a free reign using both a running commentary from the ground and the beams of searchlights to seek out their prey. These tactics had been used in moderation on previous raids but did not normally bring the success achieved by radar vectoring. The latter tactics were known as 'Tame Boar' sorties and the new method as 'Wild Boar'.

Although German records indicate that this last raid was the most devastating of the three attacks on Hamburg, presumably because the fires were so vast that accurate bombing became a simple task, it was also costly for the RAF. The freedom of attention from night fighters on the previous two raids perhaps lulled some crews into a false sense of security, and vigilance was not all it might have

Bostons of No. 88 Sqn. with BZ399/RH-E leading, about to leave their dispersals for an invasion support operation. In addition to AEAF wing stripes, each machine has washable white distemper on its nose section as an aid to identification during 'Overlord' operations.

been; 30 bombers failed to return and some that did get back carried the scars of encounters with night fighters. One of these was the Halifax of F/Off. Jenkins of No. 10 Sqn. which was attacked by a Ju88 before it reached the target. Both elevators were shot away, one tyre was punctured and the wings and fuselage damaged. After jettisoning his load, Fg. Off. Jenkins managed to shake off the Ju88, which was probably damaged by fire from the Halifax's gunners, and returned to his base at Melbourne, Yorkshire where he accomplished a successful crash-landing. The foregoing is one of the many tributes to the sometimes underrated Handley Page bomber's ability to absorb a considerable amount of damage and still stay airborne.

On 2/3 August Bomber Command made its fourth visit to Hamburg in ten days. The weather was very much against the bombers and this time the results were poor; once more night fighters were up in some strength and another 30 bombers failed to return. During this period, over 74 per cent of Hamburg was destroyed and 50,000 people were killed, a total that was only 1,000 short of the number killed in air raids on Britain throughout the whole war. Over the four raids, Bomber Command's loss rate was 2·8 per cent from 3,095 sorties, which means that if the average loss rate of the period is taken as 4·16 per cent, Window had saved forty bombers and their crews. During this concentrated effort against Hamburg, other cities had also been attacked by smaller forces, which had also used Window. Their loss rates had decreased in similar fashion.

To every measure there is a counter-measure, and the German use of Wild Boar tactics was only the start; new airborne radar which was not affected by jamming of this type was being developed, and soon the aluminium curtain would not be nearly as protective.

The intensity of the attacks on Hamburg were having the effect Harris had predicted, but although he may well have suspected this there was no way in which he could receive definite proof, since the German propaganda machine was unlikely to broadcast the fact to the free world. It was not until Albert Speer, the German armaments minister, published his memoirs, that it became generally known how close the bomber had become to being the decisive weapon. In his book,[1] Speer commented that if the RAF had extended its attacks to other major cities with campaigns similar to those mounted against the Ruhr and Hamburg, Germany might not have been able to withstand the damage inflicted.

During the Battle of Hamburg, Bomber Command's attention was turned towards Italy, which had already been raided on several occasions from bases in England. The long haul over the Alps had tested the airmanship and fortitude of many crews, especially those who had been flying the Stirling, which in many instances had skirted between the mountains rather than over them. The greater altitude capability of the Lancaster made it a much safer aircraft for such excursions, so the type was a natural choice when it came to mounting a new offensive which was now to be double-edged. With the Allies now established in North Africa, new operational airfields were available to Bomber Command, and the plan was to carry out 'shuttle-bombing' whereby the Main Force would fly from England to a selected Italian target, bomb it and fly on to North Africa, where the aircraft would be refuelled and rearmed and the next day return to England via another Italian city. This method had been tried on the night of 20/21 June when No. 5 Group Lancasters attacked Friedrichshafen then flew on to Algiers from where they returned the next day, dropping bombs on the Italian naval base at Spezia en route.

The first raid in the new series came on 7 August when Milan, Turin and Genoa were the targets, and for the next ten days Italian cities suffered as their German counterparts had. By 15 August almost half of Milan lay in ruins and over 250 industrial installations had been damaged, some of them beyond repair. The aged Stirling was used in some of the raids, and on the night of 12/13 August during an attack on Turin, F/Sgt. A. Aaron of No. 218 Sqn., became the second Stirling captain to be awarded the VC, and the only ex-Air Training Corps cadet to be so honoured. The only other Stirling VC went to F/Sgt. R. H. Middleton, RAAF, who almost a year before, on 28/29 November 1942, had received the same decoration while attacking the same target.

1. *Inside the Third Reich*; Weidenfeld & Nicolson; London, 1970.

Melsbroek, Brussels, November 1944. Bombs go out to No. 2 Group Mitchells including machines of No. 320 (Dutch) Sqn., represented by the Mk.II in the foreground. As well as AEAF markings, the aircraft bears the Dutch insignia and an impressive bomb log on the nose.

Analysis of target photographs being carried out by a squadron leader intelligence officer with the aid of an illuminated magnifier.

A Halifax Mk.III over Wanne-Eicker in the Ruhr during a daylight raid in October 1944. The camouflage pattern is shown to advantage, as is the square patch indicating the dinghy stowage on the port wing; Lancasters carried their dinghy in the starboard wing.

A No. 617 Sqn. Lancaster B.I (Special) loaded with a 22,000lb Grand Slam bomb. From left to right the crew was: F/Off. Weaver, F/Off. Barry, Flt. Lt. Sayers, F/Off. Johnson, and F/Off. Wittmer.

During the 7 August raid on Turin, Wg. Cdr. J. H. Searby had carried out a dress rehearsal for his role of Master Bomber which he undertook for the first time on 17/18 August during an attack against the experimental research station at Peenemünde. For some time intelligence reports had indicated that highly secret work was being carried out at this establishment on the development of guided missiles and it became essential that a decisive blow must be made.

A force of 597 bombers in three waves bombed three separate aiming points, approaching their target from the sea and led by a small force of Mosquitoes of No. 139 Sqn., which overflew Peenemünde and carried on to Berlin. The Mosquitoes dropped Window to create an impression that the Main Force was headed for Berlin and this spoof worked as much of the night fighter force was assembled over the German capital. When the ground controllers realized their error they called on all available forces to fly to Peenemünde, arriving in time to make concentrated attacks on the third wave. Some of the night fighters were fitted with a new weapon christened 'schräge Musik', two 30mm cannon mounted to point upwards from the fuselage. Thus armed, the pilot crept underneath an unsuspecting bomber and fired at the fuel tanks. Since there was no continually manned ventral

position in any British bomber, crew vigilance became doubly important. When the existence of 'schräge Musik' became generally known, pilots would rock their aircraft from side to side to give the mid-upper gunner a good view below.

One of the first crews to encounter a night fighter armed with schräge Musik was that of Plt. Off. T. Bishop of No. 51 Sqn. Soon after leaving the target area, Bishop banked his Halifax on to a new heading and as the aircraft turned, the mid-upper gunner, Sgt. Holder, looked down and saw a Bf110 formating below. He quickly warned Bishop, who immediately corkscrewed to starboard. As the Halifax lurched over on to its other wing tip, Holder saw a stream of fire leave the top of the Bf110 and his first reaction was that it had been hit by another

The starboard tyre of a Halifax punctured by fire from a night fighter.

bomber or was disintegrating. Sergeant Waldon, ensconced in the Halifax's rear turret, managed to get off a quick burst from his four Brownings before the Bf110 cartwheeled onto its side and dived to safety, its pilot no doubt looking for a less alert crew. It was not until the new German weapon became generally known that this crew realized just how close they had been to becoming one of the first victims.

Peenemünde was well defended by flak, and although the night fighters arrived late, they and the ground defences accounted for forty-one bombers, which was a loss rate of 6·86 per cent, and slightly above the acceptable figure, but in view of the importance of the target, a reasonable price to

A pleasing air-to-air shot of a No. 15 Sqn. Lancaster. (Author)

pay for its destruction. This raid certainly delayed the introduction into service of the V1 and especially the V2, against which there was no defence.

The approach of the long winter evenings gave Harris an opportunity to mount a series of concentrated attacks on more distant targets, and he made it quite clear that he favoured giving Berlin the same treatment that Essen and Hamburg had received during the opening phases of the Battles of the Ruhr and Hamburg. The 'Big City', as it was known to the crews, presented a different set of problems. It was beyond the range of Oboe, and would therefore have to be marked by H2S, not an ideal method, as the city's topography did not produce an ideal radar picture. It was also a modern city spread over a large area in which industry was not concentrated, and the buildings were not likely to be as inflammable as those in Hamburg or Lübeck, for example.

Berlin had been bombed many times before with varying degrees of success, but the three exploratory raids carried out over a period of one week at the end of August, brought poor results and a loss rate of over 7 per cent, so a halt was called until an improved version of H2S was available. On 3 November Harris penned to Churchill his now famous claim: 'We can wreck Berlin from end to end if the USAAF will come in on it. It will cost between 400–500 aircraft. It will cost Germany the war.' Everyone is blessed with perfect hindsight and it is now very easy for critics of the bomber offensive to continually throw Harris's words back at him, and point out that it took over a year after the main offensive finished in April 1944 for the Germans to capitulate; but evidence then available to the C-in-C strongly suggested that if Berlin could be made to suffer as other cities had, the enemy will to resist would be strongly undermined. In view of Speer's previously quoted post-war views, Harris may well have been right, and if a greater force had been available to him, his statement may well have been truly prophetic.

As it was, evidence suggests that the effort required to destroy Berlin was grossly underestimated; sixteen major raids were planned and mounted but these took a much longer period than those which had brought Hamburg and Essen to their knees. The offensive was opened on the night of 18/19 November by a force of 440 Lancasters, but a high rate of unserviceability of H2S, plus dense cloud which obscured the markers, produced poor results. Four days later 764 aircraft, included in which total were 40 Stirlings carrying out their last operational mission to Berlin, again encountered heavy cloud. However, the largest number of No. 8 Group pathfinder aircraft yet used managed to keep the target well illuminated in spite of the overcast.

41

Among the pathfinders was the first Canadian-built Halifax Mk III, operated by No. 405 Sqn., which had been transferred from No. 6 (RCAF) Group to No. 8 Group.

Berlin was well defended and new radar in the night fighters, as well as on the ground, had to a certain extent negated Window, and turned the balance back in favour of the defenders. During this period of time electronic warfare, as we know it today, was born. Although the German night fighters had now found a way through the Window jamming and had equipment which enabled them to home on to the emissions from H2S sets, they encountered many other forms of counter-measure. An increasing proportion of the bomber force was being equipped with a tail warning radar code-named 'Monica', which gave crews indication of the presence of night fighters, which in turn were hampered by other devices. One was a jammer known as 'Mandrel' and was, like many similar successful innovations, simplicity itself. A microphone buried in one of the engine cowlings of the bomber could be switched on by the wireless operator after he had tuned his set to a frequency being used by the night fighters; the effect on a night fighter pilot of having the sound of a Merlin or Hercules engine suddenly transmitted through his headset can only be imagined. 'Monica' was comparatively short-lived as it was discovered, in July 1944, that night fighters could home on it, but 'Mandrel' and 'Airborne Cigar' (ABC) served very useful purposes. ABC was particularly successful and consisted of aircraft carrying German-speaking specialists who tuned their equipment to the German night fighter frequencies and gave decoy messages to the crews. Even when the Germans discovered this and tried to counter it by using female controllers, they were not 100 per cent successful, as the RAF introduced German-speaking WAAFs, who did not fly operationally but used long-range transmitters from England.

The German night fighters also found a new menace in the form of Mosquito aircraft operating within the main stream, some of which were fitted with 'Serrate' radar which could home onto the night fighters' equipment. These aircraft, and intruders which attacked enemy airfields, certainly made life uncomfortable for the Germans, but the problem of defending a stream of bombers which could stretch over a distance of 70 miles, was still an immense one. It was not until late 1944/early 1945, when the non-availability of fuel and spares hampered the night fighters, that losses began to reduce.

Throughout the long winter months Bomber Command hammered away at targets all over Germany, but the main focus of attention was Berlin. The last raid in the proposed 'knock-out' series, came on 24/25 March 1944, but actual winds varied from the forecast and many of the 822 aircraft were scattered from the stream. This resulted in the loss of 72 bombers (9·2 per cent) an increase over the average for the battle but one which was to be surpassed five days later when 94 aircraft from a force of 795 failed to return from Nuremberg. This raid, which is usually taken as the last during the Battle of Berlin, has been well documented by aviation historians, the most comprehensive study being that by Martin Middlebrook in his excellent book.[1]

Nuremberg was Bomber Command's most disastrous effort from the loss point of view and the reason why the Main Force operated in a way contrary to tried and proved techniques has never been fully explained. Instead of making several dog-legs on the course to Nuremberg, the bombers flew direct from their bases to their first turning point at Charleroi, then a direct route of 250 miles to the target. This route took them close to two well-known night fighter beacons, and this, as well as the absence of the usual quantity of spoof raids, made interception easy for the night fighters. The weather also played an important part, with varying winds and a clear sky, whereas cloud cover had been forecast. Another phenomenon which did not help the bombers was the low level at which condensation trails formed, these making them doubly easy to find. A high proportion of the bombers lost were shot down on their way to the target, over which cloud obscured the main aiming point. The result was that very few bombs fell on Nuremberg, and damage was slight.

The final stage of area attacks on industrial cities came in April after which Bomber Command was switched to more tactical targets as a prelude to the

1. *The Nuremberg Raid*; Allen Lane; London, 1973.

invasion. The campaign, which had lasted almost exactly one year, cost the command 2,824 aircraft in a total of 75,000 sorties. Destruction of German cities and industrial complexes had been staggering, but production had not been affected to the extent hoped, for in 1944 the German aircraft industry produced more than it had in the previous two years. Nonetheless it was a worthwile effort which certainly brought home to the German people the effect of area bombing and placed them as firmly in the front line as their own leaders' actions had previously placed the citizens of London, Coventry, Southampton, Liverpool and other cities. The fact that German civilians displayed the same resilience and fortitude probably goes a long way to explaining why the offensive did not produce the anticipated results.

TACTICAL OPERATIONS

From the beginning of the war until mid-1943, when the new heavy four-engined bombers started to become available in considerable quantities, Bomber Command had relied on twin-engined aircraft such as the Whitley, Hampden, Manchester and Wellington. Although the heavies sounded the death knell of the lighter twins as strategic bombers,

A pathfinder Mosquito about to receive its 4,000lb 'Cookie'. The marriage of pathfinder techniques to the finest light bomber extant was one of the greatest single factors in the successful conclusion of the bomber offensive. (Fox Photos)

there was still a place for such aircraft in a tactical rôle, using newer types.

No. 2 Group (Blenheim squadrons of which had made the first bombing raids of WWII) stayed part of Bomber Command until May 1943 when it left to form part of the 2nd Tactical Air Force. During its time with Bomber Command, No. 2 Group was mainly equipped with American-manufactured aircraft such as the Boston, Ventura and Mitchell, which it used to carry out short-range daylight operations against targets in Europe, supported by Fighter Command, in the period when efforts were being made to carry the fight to the enemy. The work of the Blenheims and Bostons was confined mainly to the 1942 period, by the end of which both were becoming rather outclassed for the tasks set them. In late 1942 the Lockheed Ventura, which had started to equip No. 21 Sqn. during the summer, was ready for operations, the first being against Henglo on 3 November. A month later on 6 December, 47 Venturas from Nos. 21, 464 (RAAF) and 487 (RNZAF) Sqns. formed part of a force detailed to attack the Philips factory at Eindhoven. The attack was pressed home from low level through a heavy curtain of accurate anti-aircraft

Pilot and navigator climb aboard their Mosquito for another strike on Berlin, 22 March 1945. (Fox Photos)

fire. Nine of the new American bombers failed to return and 37 were damaged—not an auspicious start for an aircraft from which much was hoped. Unfortunately this proved to be the pattern of events for the Ventura and although the type took part in 'Circus' and 'Ramrod' operations, mainly carried out at high level, limitations were critical.

On 3 May, No. 487 Sqn. was detailed for a raid on a power-station in Amsterdam and briefed to press home the attack irrespective of opposition. Led by Sqn. Ldr. L. Trent, the two formations of Venturas approached the Dutch coast at low level then climbed to altitude for their bomb-run. They were immediately intercepted by a force of over 70 Bf109s and Fw190s, the latter concentrating on the Venturas' Spitfire escort whilst the former picked off the bombers. Of the 11 aircraft which had set out, only 2, flown by Sqn. Ldr. Trent and his number 2, succeeded in reaching the target, and they were both shot down shortly after bombing.

The only aircraft to return to its base was that flown by Flt. Lt. A. Duffill, which had been attacked during the first interception and severely damaged. For his leadership on this raid Sqn. Ldr. Trent received the VC. In July both Nos. 487 and 464 Sqns. stood down from operations but No. 21 Sqn. continued to operate the Ventura until September when it, like the other two, converted to Mosquitoes.

It was in the Mosquito that Bomber Command found the ideal twin-engined bomber aircraft. Used as a night fighter, intruder, and photographic reconnaissance aircraft, as well as a bomber, the Mosquito's contribution to WWII was considerable. In it Bomber Command had an aircraft that was virtually impossible to intercept and as well as using it in the pathfinder role, formed a Light Night Striking Force within No. 8 Group. On nights that the Main Force could not operate, the LNSF roamed far and wide over Germany, delivering bombs up to 4,000lb capacity, in nuisance raids which kept the defences on constant stand-by. Mosquito bombers dropped 26,867 tons of bombs in 28,639 sorties and completed a total of 39,795 sorties during service with Bomber Command, a not inconsiderable achievement for an aircraft which started out as a private venture and for which the RAF originally had no requirement.

During the build-up to the invasion of Europe, Bomber Command was used to attack communication systems, troop concentrations and other targets, the destruction of which would hinder the enemy's ability to counter the proposed landings. On 'D-Day' itself, 16 Lancasters of No. 617 Sqn. led by Grp. Capt. L. Cheshire flying LM482—'W' for Whiskey—co-operated with a small force of ships in a spoof raid which was aimed at convincing the Germans that the main landings were to be in the Calais area.

The Lancasters flew a systematic pattern in which they doubled back over their track and continually dropped Window. The result was the appearance on German radar of a trace which seemed to indicate a slow moving seaborne force. Meanwhile, prior to the landings, Oboe-equipped Mosquitoes of Nos. 105 and 109 Sqns. led a huge force of Halifaxes and Lancasters against the heavy gun emplacements on the Normandy coast. Stirlings of Nos. 218 and 149 Sqns. flew similar missions to that of No. 617's

Lancasters, and some of No. 149 Sqn.'s aircraft together with Halifaxes of Nos. 138 and 161 Sqns. dropped dummy paratroops near Yvetot. Four days after the Allied landings, No. 617 Sqn. employed its specially developed precision methods to attack the Saumur tunnel using another of Dr. Barnes Wallis's weapons, the 12,000lb 'Tallboy' earthquake bomb, for the first time.

Although attacks were resumed against the German homeland, Bomber Command was still ready to support the ground forces whenever it was required to do so. Typical tactical strikes were made by No. 3 Group Lancasters and No. 4 Group Halifaxes on enemy positions around Caen on 30 June, followed on 7 and 18 July by attacks on enemy positions and the suburbs of the city by 457 and 2,000 aircraft, respectively. Several more raids were required in this area before a hole was punched in the enemy defences. A vital rôle was played by Bomber Command in the capture of Channel ports where the garrisons showed commendable fortitude under the severe bombardments they endured.

During the prelude to the invasion, Bomber Command had been controlled by the Supreme Allied Commander but in September 1944 this control passed to the Chief of Air Staff for a new campaign aimed primarily at oil and transportation systems. From October 1944 casualty rates began to fall quite dramatically, principally because large areas of Europe were falling into Allied hands and depriving the Luftwaffe of airfields and ground radar control, but also because of the efforts of No. 100 Group, which was becoming specialized in feint raids, jamming of enemy radar and general countermeasure activities.

Raids by over 1,000 bombers now became fairly commonplace with Duisburg receiving two on successive nights on 14–16 October for the loss of only 21 aircraft. Ten days later, a combined force of 199 Halifaxes, 32 Lancasters and 12 Mosquitoes attacked the synthetic oil plant at Hamburg without loss—which was a far different story from that of the previous year.

On 12 November a force of 29 Lancasters from Nos. 9 and 617 Sqns. finally succeeded in removing a thorn that had plagued Bomber Command since the earliest days of the war, when it sank the German battleship *Tirpitz* in Alten Fjord. With Allied air superiority growing daily, Bomber Command was able to operate with a higher degree of safety during daylight hours and 15 of 20 attacks on the Ruhr between October and December were such raids.

The early months of 1945 saw a tremendous increase in the tempo of operations, 40 raids being mounted in February alone. Among them was the infamous destruction of Dresden on the night of the 13/14th, which was also bombed the following day by the USAAF. In March there were 53 day and night operations, one of the heaviest being on the 11th when a force of over 1,000 bombers dropped 4,680 tons in the fifteenth massed raid on Essen; but tactical rather than strategic targets were now becoming more the order of the day, with U-boat

Loading a 22,000lb bomb aboard a No. 617 Sqn. Lancaster at Woodhall Spa.

pens, railway marshalling yards, bridges and viaducts featuring prominently. The first 22,000lb 'Grand Slam' bomb was used against the Bielefeld viaduct on 14 March and this raid was followed by others on the 15th and 19th in preparation for the Ruhr crossing.

One of the last raids which captured the public imagination was carried out on 25 April when 318 Lancasters attempted to destroy Hitler's hideaway in Bavaria, where Neville Chamberlain had signed

Carrying yellow G-H formation leader's bars on its fins, this Lancaster is NG358/H of No. 15 Sqn., Mildenhall, mid-1945.

the Munich Agreement in 1938. The small target presented the crews with a difficult problem and it escaped damage; nonetheless the relish with which it was undertaken no doubt more than compensated for its failure, since it was felt that a personal blow was being carried out against the *Führer*.

On 2/3 May 1945 Bomber Command aircraft operated for the last time, carrying out a total of 303 sorties against Kiel, Eggebeck and Husum airfields, the forces involved comprising Mosquitoes, Halifaxes, Liberators and Fortresses.

When the cease-fire finally came, many of the bombers returned to Germany to help in the repatriation of PoWs, and also took ground crews on what became known as 'Cook's Tours' of the bombed cities and industrial areas. This was an inspired gesture, and gave the often overlooked but vitally important ground crews a view of the damage they had helped to create. Without these men and women who kept the bomber stations functioning and serviced the aircraft in all types of weather and sometimes under difficult conditions, the bomber offensive could never have been carried out. This fact is all too frequently overlooked when it comes to the final analysis of the defeat of Germany in which everyone in Bomber Command played a vital part.

THE AIRCRAFT

Avro Lancaster
Developed from the Manchester, the Lancaster became the mainstay of Bomber Command. A total of 7,377 were built and 3,345 were lost in action. Lancasters flew 156,318 sorties and dropped 608,613 tons of bombs.

Wingspan 102ft *Length* 69ft 6in *Height* 20ft *Weight loaded* 68,000lb or 70,000lb with a 22,000lb bomb *Weight empty* 36,900lb *Armament* Eight ·303in Browning machine guns in nose, tail and mid-upper turrets; some aircraft fitted with two MGs in ventral turret; bomb load 14,000lb normal, 22,000lb maximum *Powerplant* Four Rolls-Royce Merlin 20, 22 or 24 *Maximum speed* 287mph at 11,500ft *Cruising speed* 210mph *Ceiling* 24,500ft

Handley Page Halifax B.Mk III
Sharing most of the wartime bombing effort with the Lancaster, the Halifax flew a total of 83,138 sorties and dropped 224,407 tons of bombs. Of the 5,797 Halifaxes built as bombers, 1,935 were lost in action.

Wingspan 104ft 2in *Length* 71ft 7in *Height* 20ft 9in *Weight loaded* 65,000lb *Weight empty* 37,240lb *Armament* One ·303in Vickers K machine gun in nose cone; eight ·303in Brownings in mid-upper and tail turrets; some aircraft fitted with a single ventral ·50in Browning MG; bomb load 13,000lb

in fuselage bomb bay and wing cells *Powerplant*
Four Bristol Hercules XVI radials *Maximum speed*
281mph at 13,500ft *Cruising speed* 210mph *Ceiling*
20,000ft.

Some went home intact. Home was a long way from the devastation of Europe for Lancaster X KB670/NA-P of No. 428 (Ghost) Sqn., RCAF. Just one example of a well-decorated Canadian Lanc, this machine also carried the name 'P-for Panic' on the starboard side of the nose and other feelingly applied slogans on the fuselage. Each engine was also named, the port inner being 'Passionate'. (National Museum of Science & Technology, Ottawa)

Notes sur les planches en couleur

Page 25: *Flight Lieutenant, Royal Australian Air Force*, 1944, mis en tenue de service normal en la couleur distinctive de bleue foncée australienne. L'insigne doré d'un Albatros dessus de grade sur manchette fut aussi une singularité nationale, de même dessin comme insigne de calot. Dessous de brevet de pilote sur le sein gauche, il porte cordons de *Distinguished Flying Cross* et de *Air Force Cross*.

Page 26 dessus: Short Stirling B.Mk III EF452 of No. 218 (Gold Coast) Sqn., No. 3 Group, Downham Market, Suffolk, août 1943. Cet avion fut volé de F/Sgt. A. Aaron la nuit du 12/13 août, un vol à Turin qui aboutit à la récompense de la deuxième *Victoria Cross* au capitaine Stirling. Cet avion porte dessin de camouflage 4 en les couleurs de Terre Foncée/Verte Foncée sur les hautes surfaces avec 'Noire à Nuit' sur les côtés en bas, rondelles sur fuselage étantes 54in en diamètre Type C1, rondelles sur escadres 75in en diamètre Type B. Lettres en chiffre furent 4ft en hauteur sur le Stirling avec numéros de série 8in en hauteur.

Page 26 dessous: Avro Lancaster B.Mk III ED680 of No. 61 Sqn., No. 5 Group, Skellingthorpe, Lincs, 1944. Illustré comme il fut après 118 sorties de campagne, ce Lancaster fut péri dans un accident pendant décollage la nuit du 28/29 octobre, 1944, en faisant partir au raid aérien à Bergen. Son 100ème vol fut fait le 27/28 juin 1944, une sortie à Vitry-La-François avec F/Lt. B. Turner aux leviers de commande. En camouflage normal de commandement des avions de bombardement, le registre de sorties d'avion fut présenté comme files de dix symboles de bombes, la 106ème sortie étante indiquée en forme de la silhouette d'une 4,000lb 'Cookie'.

Page 27: De Havilland Mosquito B.Mk IV DK333 of No. 109 Sqn., No. 8 Group PFF, Wyton, Hunts, 1944. Peindu en couleur de camouflage normal pour avions de bombardement avec Vert de Verte Foncée et Grise Océanique sur les hautes surfaces avec Noir à Nuit sur les côtés de dessous, l'avion ont été illustré après 29 opérations. Comme pour les gros avions de bombardement, Mosquitoes déployèrent souvent 'art distinctif sur le nez' contigu à leurs registres de campagne, la figure de 'Grim Reaper' étant très appropriée à l'offensive d'avions de bombardement. Rondelles sur fuselage de Mosquitoes furent 36in en diamètre Type C1, avec 54in en diamètre Type B sur les escadres.

Pages 28–29: Handley Page Halifax B.Mk II Series Ia HR946, No. 51 Sqn., No. 4 Group, Snaith, Yorkshire, novembre 1943. Distribué à No. 51 Sqn. en juillet 1943, HR946 resta dans cette fraction jusqu'à janvier 1944 quand il fut transporté à No. 77 Sqn. à Elvington pour devenir KN-X. Fini en camouflage normal de Terre Foncée/Verte Foncée Noir à Nuit, l'avion tint rondelles sur fuselage Type C1 54in en diamètre et rondelles sur escadre Type B 95in en diamètre, lettres en chiffre 4ft en hauteur et numéros de série 8in en hauteur. L'art montre le Halifax comme il fut l'après-midi du 10 novembre, 1943, au moment avant son 15ème vol, une sortie à Cannes cette nuit. Une silhouette d'une 15ème bombe fut entrée dans le livre de bord l'après-midi du 11 novembre, l'equipage ayant laissé tomber par terre coquelicots sur France pendant son retour de Cannes dans une action non officielle aux Français pour marquer le 11 novembre.

Page 30: Handley Page Halifax B.Mk VII NP763 of No. 346 'Guyenne' Sqn., French Air Force, No. 4 Group, Elvington, Yorks, 1944–45. Une de deux escadrilles Halifax armée de personnel français, les appareils de No. 346 tinrent leurs rondelles sur fuselage 'renversées' dans l'ordre de marquages français nationaux et ils portèrent les marquages distinctifs sur l'empennage appliqués à plusieures escadrilles de Groupe No. 4 RAF dans le but d'identification de vols de jour. Cet avion montre aussi les contours jaunes de lettres en chiffre avec la lettre individuelle d'avion répétée sur les dérives.

Page 31 dessus: Une sélection d'insignes et de marquages. (A) Marquage personnel de Halifax B.Mk III LV860/KW-U de No. 425 Sqn., RCAF. (B) Marquage personnel de Lancaster B.III PB532/HW-S^2, No. 100 Sqn., avril 1945. Le nom fut issu d'origines sud-américaines du pilote, Flt. Lt. O. Lloyd-Davies. (C) Insignes déployèrent de plusieurs Mosquitoes de No. 105 Sqn. (D) Marquage d'empennage de Lancaster B.III of No. 97 (Straits Settlements) Sqn., août 1944. (E) Marquages indiquants un Lancaster d'un chef G–H. (F) Marquage d'empennage Halifax B.VI, No. 102 Sqn. (G) Marquage d'empennage, Halifax B.III, No. 462 Sqn., RAAF. (H) Exemples de marquages des avions de bombardement utilisés pour registrer les opérations volées et les médailles remportées—en ce cas la DFC (blanche/pourpre) et DSO (rouge/bleue). (I) Marquage en craie, Halifax B.III MZ714/KW-Y, No. 425 Sqn., RCAF—troisième file de 25 symboles de bombes n'est pas illustrée.

Page 31 dessous: Ambulance avec marquage sur garde-boue indiquant un véhicule utilisé de No. 3 Group et une plaque de numéro minéralogique typique.

Page 32 gauche: *Air gunner*, 1944, mis en vêtements d'aviateur avec casque d'aviateur récent Type C attaché avec du fil de métal. Le dolman Irvin de basane et pantalon qui vont ensemble, sont portés avec bottes 'd'évasion': les tiges de suède purent être étées en cas d'urgence, les pieds ressemblants souliers civils. L'harnais de parachute est porté sur la ceinture de sauvetage dégonflée et un paquetage de parachute est porté.

Page 32 droit: *Flight Sergeant* d'une Polish escadrille, 1943–44, mis en tenue de service avec les deux insignes de RAF et de *Polish Air Force*. L'insigne de calot des autres grades RAF; pièce d'épaule en force d'un Albatros des autres grades RAF avec 'POLAND' dessus de motif; bouton polonais dessus de chevrons de RAF; et pièces de grade polonaises sur col de dentelle d'or sur étoffe bleue de RAF.

Farbtafeln

Seite 25: *Flight Lieutenant, Royal Australian Air Force*, 1944, auf normaler Dienstfrackuniform in der kennzeichnenden australischen dunkel-blauen Farbe. Abzeichen eines vergoldeten Albatroses ober Stulpedienstgrad war auch eine nationale Eigenheit, von gliechem Entwurf als Feldmützeabzeichen. Unter Titularrang Pilots auf linker Brust trägt er Ordensbände *Distinguished Flying Cross* und *Air Force Cross*.

Seite 26 oben: Short Stirling B.Mk III EF452 of No. 218 (Gold Coast) Sqn., No. 3 Group, Downham Market, Suffolk, August 1943. Dies Flugzeug wurde an der Nacht 12/13 August von F/Sgt. A. Aaron auf einem Einsatz nach Turin geführt, dem zur Folge die Auszeichnung des zweiten *Victoria Cross* zu einem Stirling-Hauptflugzeugführer hatte. Das Flugzeug trägt dunkelerdiges/dunkelgrünes Tarnungsmuster 4 auf den Oberflächen mit 'Nacht-Schwarz' auf den Unterseiten, runde Rumpfscheiben sind 54in im Durchmesser Type C1, runde Tragflächescheiben 75in im Durchmesser Type B. Verschlüsselte Buchstaben ware 4ft hoch auf dem Stirling mit Seriennummern 8in hoch.

Seite 26 unten: Avro Lancaster B.Mk III ED680 of No. 61 Sqn., No. 5 Group, Skellingthorpe, Lincs, 1944. Illustriert als es nach 118 Operationseinsätze war, wurde dies Lancaster am Nacht 28/29 October 1944 in einem Abflugumfall abgebucht, als es sich für einem Angriff nach Bergen Machte auf. Sein 100ter Flug wurde am 27/28 Juni 1944 gemacht, der im Einsatz mit F/Lt. B. Turner am Steuerknüppel nach Vitry-La-François war. Auf Tarnung Normalbomberführung wurde die Einsatzaufzeichnung wie Reihen zehn Bombezeichen vorgestellt, der 106te Einsatz wurde von einem Schattenbild einer 4,000lb 'Cookie' illustriert.

Seite 27: De Havilland Mosquito B.Mk IV DK333 of No. 109 Sqn., No. 8 Group PFF, Wyton, Hunts, 1944. Angestrichen in der Farbe Normaltarnung eines Tagesbombenflugzeugs Dunkelgrün und 'Meeresgrau' auf den Oberflächen mit 'Nachtschwarz' auf den Unterseiten hat man das Flugzeug nach Erfüllung 29 Operations illustriert. Wie mit schweren Bombern zeigten Mosquitoes Kennzeichende 'Bugkunst' anliegend an seinen Operationsaufzeichnungen, die Gelstalt des 'Grim Reaper' war nur zu zuständig zu dem Bomberangriff. Runde Rumpfscheiben auf Mosquitoes waren 36in im Durchmesser Type C1, mit 54in im Durchmesser Type B auf den Tragflächen.

Seiten 28–29: Handley Page Halifax B.Mk II Series Ia HR946, No. 51 Sqn., No. 4 Group, Snaith, Yorkshire, November 1943. Ausgegeben zu No. 51 Sqn. im Juli 1943 blieb HR 946 bei diesem Verband bis January 1944, als es nach No. 77 Sqn. in Elvington verlegt wurde, wo es KN-X wurde. Mit einem Deckanstrich dunkelerdiger/dunkelgrüner/nachtschwarzer Normaltarnung hatte das Flugzeug runde Rumpfscheiben 54in im Durchmesser Type C1 und runde Tragflächescheiben 95in im Durchmesser Type B, verschlüsselte Buchstaben 4ft Höhe und Seriennummern 8in Höhe. Die Kunstarbeit zeigt das Halifax wie es am Nachmittag 10 November 1943 gerade vorhergehend zeinem 15th Flug war, im Einsatz an dieser Nacht mach Cannes. Ein 15th Bombenschattenbild wurde am Nachmittag 11 Novembers in das Bordbuch gesetzt, und das Flugpersonal entliess Mohne, über Frankreich, als sie von Cannes

zurückfuhr, die eine inoffizielle Geste zu den Franzosen war, um Gedächtnistag zu markieren.

Seite 30: Handley Page Halifax B.Mk VII NP763 of No. 346 'Guyenne' Sqn., French Air Force, No. 4 Group, Elvington, Yorks, 1944–45 eine von zwei Halifax-Staffeln von französischem Personal besetzt wurde das Flugzeuge No. 346. No. 346 ihre runde Rumpfscheiben in der Reihenfolge französscher Staatshoheitsabzeichen umgekehrt und sie trugen die kennzeichende Rumpfendehoheitsabzeichen, die zu einer Anzahl Staffeln in Nummer 4 Gruppe RAF für Kennabsichten auf Tagesoperationen aufgetragen wurden. Dies Flugzeug zeigt auch gelbe scharf abgehobene verschlüsselte Buchstaben mit dem Einzelbuchstabe des Flugzeugs wieder auf den Flossen aufgetragen.

Seite 31 oben: Eine Auswahl Abzeichen und Hoheitsabzeichen (A) Persönliches Abzeichen Halifax B.Mk III LV 860/KW-U of No. 425 Sqn., RCAF. (B) Persönliches Abzeuchen Lancaster B.III PB532/HW-S², No. 100 Sqn., April 1945. Der Name stammte von dem südamerikanischen Ursprung des Pilots, Flt. Lt. O. Lloyd-Davies. (C) Abzeichen zeigten von einer Anzahl Mosquitoes No. 105 Sqn. (D) Rumpfendeabzeichen Lancaster B.III of No. 97 (Straits Settlements) Sqn., August, 1944. (D) Abzeichen bezeichnen ein Lancaster eines G-H Führer. (E) Rumpfendeabzeichen, Halifax B.VI, No. 102 Sqn. (F) Rumpfendeabzeichen Halifax B.III, No. 462 Sqn., RAAF. (G) Beispiele Hoheitsabzeichen Bombers, die angewendet wurden, um Operations geführt und Ordnen getragen aufgezeichnet—in diesem Fall die DFC (weiss/purpurn) und DSO (rot/blau). (H) Kreideabzeichen, Halifax B.III MZ714/KW-Y, No. 425 Sqn., RCAF—dritte Reihe 25 Bombezeichen nicht illustriert.

Seite 31 unten: Bomber Command Austin K2 Krankenwagen mit Kotflügelabzeichen das ein Wagen von No. 3 Group angewendet und ein typisches Nummernschild zeigt.

Seite 32 links: *Air gunner*, 1944, auf voller Fliegerschutzkleidung mit spät Type C Drahtfliegerhelm bekleidet. Die Irvin-Jacke und zusammenpassende Hose sind mit 'Escape'-Stiefeln: die Schäfte aus Wildleder konnte man im Notfalle ausziehen und die Füsse ähnelten Zivilschuhe. Der Fallschirmgurt wird über dem unaufblasbaren Rettungsgürtel getragen, und ein Fallschirmpack wird getragen.

Seite 32 rechts: *Flight Sergeant* einer Polish Staffel, 1943–44, auf Dienstuniform mit beiden RAF und *Polish Air Force* Abzeichen. Mützenabzeichen RAF anderen Dienstgrade; Achselrosen RAF anderen Dienstgrade mit 'POLAND' oder Leitmotiv; polnischen Knopf oder RAF-Winkeln; und polnische Dienstgradrockkragenstücke goldener Spitze auf RAF blauem Stoff.

AIRWAR SERIES

First 20 titles:

1 RAF Fighter Units, Europe, 1939–42
2 USAAF Heavy Bomber Units, ETO & MTO, 1942–45
3 Spanish Civil War Air Forces
4 Luftwaffe Ground Attack Units, 1939–45
5 RAF Bomber Units, 1939–42
6 Luftwaffe Fighter Units, Europe, 1939–41
7 USAAF Medium Bomber Units, ETO & MTO, 1942–45
8 USAAF Fighter Units, Europe, 1942–45
9 Luftwaffe Night Fighter Units, 1939–45
10 RAF Fighter Units, Europe, April 1942–45
11 Luftwaffe Fighter Units, Russia, 1941–45
12 USAAF Fighter Units, MTO, 1942–45
13 German Fighter Units, 1914–May 1917
14 British Fighter Units, Western Front, 1914–16
15 Luftwaffe Bomber Units, 1939–41
16 US Navy Carrier Air Groups, Pacific, 1941–45
17 German Fighter Units, June 1917–1918
18 British Fighter Units, Western Front, 1917–18
19 RAF Bomber Units, July 1942–1945
20 Luftwaffe Fighter Units, Mediterranean, 1941–44

Planned titles:

Japanese Carrier Air Groups, 1941–45
USAAF Bomber Units, Pacific, 1941–45
RAF Combat Units, SEAC, 1941–45
Luftwaffe Fighter Units, Europe, 1942–45